REMARKABLE TALES OF

CATS

WHO WHISPER TO HUMANS

SIGNE A. DAYHOFF, PH.D.

Remarkable Tales of Cats
Who Whisper To Humans

By Signe A. Dayhoff, PhD

Copyright © 2015 by Signe A. Dayhoff, PhD

Published by Effectiveness-Plus Publications LLC
80 Paseo de San Antonio
Placitas, New Mexico 87043-8735

Cat photo of "Smoochie and Friend" by Signe Dayhoff
Front cover design by randolene at fiverr.com
Rear cover design by around86 at fiverr.com

ISBN: 978-0-9910965-9-6

Disclaimer: This book is sold with the understanding that the publisher is not engaged in rendering psychological or any other professional service. The instruction, ideas, and advice are not intended as a substitute for medical or psychological counseling. The reader should consult a professional to determine the nature of their problem. The author and publisher disclaim any responsibility or liability resulting from application of procedures presented or discussed in this book.

DEDICATION

This book is dedicated to all cats, homeless or otherwise, and to their humans who have felt the impact of these mysterious cat human-whispering skills. It is through these skills that cats have influenced the creation of human-cat relationships. The previously untold stories in this volume were shared by the cats who lived them in order that more humans could become aware of how sensitivity to human-cat communication is necessary to enhance cat lives and human-cat relationships.

I extend my undying gratitude to all cat shelter managers, especially Dr. Barbara Bayer of non-profit, no-kill CARMA, and volunteers, like Vicky Morris-Dueer, who do the impossible to save all homeless companion animals.

And I express my heartfelt gratitude to those caring and savvy cats who saw the importance of breaking their silence and coming out to altruistically contribute to this book by telling their very personal human-whispering stories.

TABLE OF CONTENTS

CHAPTER 1

WHAT IS A CAT HUMAN-WHISPERER?

Cat Human-Whisperers are felines who whisper to humans. They communicate with humans in special ways to influence the humans' behavior toward this particular cat and cats in general. This communication can take many forms. But it starts with cats' innate empathy, self-awareness, and social intelligence which allow them to see, hear, sense, experience, interpret, and know based on the direct and indirect "signs."

These human signs include behavior, personality, feelings, psychological status, perspectives, and viewpoints about issues affecting the human and cat. Both verbal and nonverbal types of communication are necessary and sufficient in most situations. Specifically, they make the connection stronger and influence human-initiated relationship changes. These are beneficial to both humans and cats and their pending relationship.

Cat Human-Whisperers seek out those who emanate an "aura" of positive energy. Then they begin "communication" by getting the humans' attention and insisting that they focus and listen. When cats feel they have opened the communication channel, they "talk heart-to-heart" with humans both verbally and nonverbally, using every sensory modality they possess. According to German philosopher Martin Buber, "An animal's eyes have the power to speak a great language."

They attempt communication primarily with those who radiate pro-cat attitudes. Intuitively they understand that getting through to humans is not always easy, especially where the human may harbor any cat-negative beliefs. This change process would require first transforming humans' beliefs from negative to positive. It is important to note that from these beliefs come human thoughts and then words. From words come actions which often turn into repetitive actions, or habits. Habits ultimately become humans' values which then go on to shape their lives. Initiating change with cat-negative humans is a long, often unrewarding exercise. As a consequence, cats clearly only seek out only those humans who show focused awareness, sensitivity, empathy, and openness to cats.

There is no "right way" for cat Human-Whisperers to talk with humans. Whatever works for the individual feline essentially "works." Cats have to use both their intuition and analytical skills to decide if what they are doing is worth the time and effort. Cats' success as Human-Whisperers begins with their using their hard-wired and finely-honed abilities to locate humans who are most amenable to cat influence. The result of this positive influence is humans who can and do sense and reflect what their cats are thinking and how they are feeling.

According to Faust, the feline subject of the memoir "What Faust the Dancing Taught Me," "We cats can sense how humans feel about us. By the time we have established communication and a relationship with a human, we *know* what's going on emotionally and physically with that person. Whether they know it or not, humans, especially those close to us, are fairly transparent about their thoughts, feelings, beliefs, and attitudes. They tell us what they know, want, and need. When we cats make changes in our lives that are in harmony with our humans' behavior, energy level, emotional state, and health, our humans will change in a similar fashion. It's all about empathy, communication, respect, and mutual benefit."

All cats have this ability to assist their humans to intuitively understand what their cat companion's needs and wants are. As a result, humans can become so highly-attuned to their feline that they *just know* when their cat is not themselves—is emotionally distressed or unwell—even though every unconnected human around them seems to think the cat is fine.

Cat Human-Whisperers achieve this connection with humans by creating a safe bridge of open communication through which the human is invited to be heard and understood in a loving and non-judgmental exchange. Once this connection is established, cat Human-Whisperers can then immediately share information with their humans. This communication lets the human:

- Know how the cat really feels
- Understand the cat's likes, dislikes, needs, dreams, and desires
- Understand the cat's behaviors from the *cat's* point of view
- Resolve behavioral or emotional challenges facing the cat and human
- Hear the cat's views about what works for them and what needs change
- Deepen their understanding of, and emotional connection with, their cat
- Become alert to and reassure the cat of forthcoming changes that will impact the cat and human
- Share cognitive, affective, and sensory messages of unconditional love.

Of course, to reiterate, all of this requires that humans be aware, open to listening and understanding, and care about establishment of communication between humans and cats in a *simpatico* relationship.

Even the most laid-back cat appreciates a focused, aware, and mindful human. Forgetful humans can be influenced to remember to provide clean, cool water daily, de-divot the litter pan several times a day, offer protein and amino-acid-balanced foods, and not raise their voice around the delicate hearing of the cat. The secret is disciplined awareness, affection, and clear communication. *The cat Human-Whisperer is ready to share if the human is ready to care.*

There are five basic requirements for cat-human communication to be effective:

Be calm. Cat Human-Whisperers should never direct or reprimand their humans when the cat is feeling angry, stressed, or fearful. It's the same for humans. Even though humans tend to be generally unaware of others, the human can often sense pique. Feeling the strong feline emotion, humans may resist following instruction, even reflecting the cat's negative emotional state. Consequently, when cats are feeling frustrated, they should take a break, chew some rye grass, roll in catnip, or climb their cat tree. Unlike humans, when cats show their feelings, they are not being dishonest, deceptive, or reflecting hidden agendas. Humans likewise need to step back, assess the situation, and acknowledge that cats may resist what seem to them like arbitrary human instructions that don't obviously benefit the cat.

Keep ahead. In order to survive humans, cats need to stay one step ahead of their humans. Because humans tend not to be all that aware of their immediate environments and are easily distracted, cats must step into the void to help guide humans progressively. To survive cats, then, humans must recognize how cats think, what they experience emotionally, and act directly to achieve their cat's goals. Once humans know how and where to look, humans will see that with cats "What you see is what you get."

Forget punishment. Cats will not tolerate verbal or physical punishment. In this regard, humans are no different. Punishment makes cats fearful, angry, and likely to over-retaliate against their punisher. Neither cats nor humans handle stress well. Humans tend to aggress when stressed while cats tend to become fearful which can morph into aggression when approached. Cats can't call for mediation when a problem looms overhead so it's up to humans to step back, analyze the situation, and objectively determine ways to calmly resolve it.

Reward their good behavior with praise. Behavior modification with any sentient being—cat or human—begins with reinforcing the positive and extinguishing the negative. When cats know what their humans like, they use that to keep their humans in a good and receptive mood. Humans bond with cats by providing what the cat likes, whether food, treats, playing, or petting. Extinguishing negative behavior can be as simple as distracting cats from it and *not* rewarding that behavior with immediate petting or soothing talk. Extinguishing negative behavior in humans works the same way. While distraction is often more difficult for cats to achieve in humans, leaving the situation quickly demonstrates that the cat does not want it to continue.

Be patient. It will take a while to influence humans' behavior because they frequently tend to be distracted with daydreaming, multi-tasking, electronic gadgets, TV, and ingesting salty, greasy, or sugary foods and intoxicating drink. So it is better to think of assisting humans by way of daily communication in focused time segments over a long period of time.

Again, it is important to note that cats are not humans. Cat behavior is not human behavior. Cats and humans work on different circadian rhythms, different needs and wants, and have totally different conceptions of time. Most of the time cats are not in as big hurry as are humans. Being aware of, understanding, and accommodating the differences are necessary for communication. These are essential for any relationship—humans and cats or humans and humans—in order to develop, grow, and blossom.

Cat Human-Whisperers have to deal with the eternal pejorative mythology of cats even when their humans have their fingers of consciousness on the pulse of cat behavior and their cat-human relationship. Humans have heard over and over throughout their lifetime erroneous so-called facts and negative opinions about felines. Even the most loving human may have concerns, resulting from these myths—erroneous beliefs—about cats in general.

As natural Human-Whisperers, cats can and must help their humans gain a deeper understanding of not only their individual cat but also cats in general in order to dispel these harmful beliefs. Specifically, cat Human-Whispers need to demonstrate to their humans that

- Cats are a different species from humans and don't think or act like humans
- Cats are a different species from dogs, don't think or act like dogs
- Cats do not need human approval but enjoy it in a relationship
- Cats do not need humans for safety, security, or protection
- Cats have social preferences and close relationships
- Cats are always themselves—but this doesn't mean selfish, aloof, or self-absorbed—just different and independent as part of their survival mechanism
- Cats expect to be respected and treated with dignity
- Cats are not evil—unlike people, they do not kill for sport, lie, or play mind games
- Cats *are* secretive about their health but *only* because it makes them less vulnerable to predation in the wild
- Cats have an innate curiosity that makes them explore and discover the world
- Cats like high places for safety and communicating with humans on an equal footing
- Cats are independent decision makers who choose to or not to live with humans
- Cats do not necessarily experience "separation anxiety" when separated from their humans but may experience the stress of change which they don't like
- Cats stay with humans because they *want* to, not because they have to
- Cats have individual, distinct, and special personalities
- Cats are hated by some humans because they do not match the expectation of a toy-like "pet"
- Cats are hated by some because they are not servile, do not do humans' bidding unless they choose to, do not conform, and are not easily manipulated
- Cats will not tolerate abuse as dogs may do
- Cats aggress only when hurt, ill, frightened, angry, or seeking prey food
- Cats primarily use their bodies, tails, ears, whiskers, and eyes to communicate

- Cats use teeth and claws to make their points because they cannot express otherwise to humans what they do not like or do not want them to do
- Cats communicate subtly allowing aware, caring, observant humans to decipher their messages
- Cats enjoy physical, emotional, and spiritual—even "psychic"—connection with humans on their own terms
- Cats form strong relationship bonds with many species of animals, including humans
- Cats do not care about human age, gender, sexual orientation, mobility, state of physical, social, or financial health—they are equal opportunity companions
- Cats like touch, especially hugging, and want to and will share it with anyone who appears to be trustworthy and positive about cats
- Cats tend to be solitary animals though they may be part of natural or artificial groups. So if they *choose* to have a relationship with humans, cats are sacrificing some of their independence in order to share their life with those humans.

By employing cat Human-Whisperer's skills, cats can discover why their human acts differently around particular people, locations, animals, or situations. If cats can understand where the behavior comes from and why, they may choose to work with humans rather than abandoning them, thus demonstrating patience, tolerance, and a willingness to work things out.

§ § §

CHAPTER 2

COMMUNICATING WITH THE HUMAN

The most important thing for cats in developing their cat-human communication skills is to use their ability to listen with all their cat senses. Cats must begin the process by getting in touch with their own intuition and allowing themselves to really feel what the human is feeling. Every cat has this natural ability. Humans have it when younger. But as humans grow older, they seem to lose that sensitivity, awareness, and mindfulness, moving away from listening to focusing on their own thoughts, beliefs, and intuition. Cats, on the other hand, continue to exercise it and build on it.

It usually takes cat Human-Whisperers to help humans fully resurrect, revitalize, and employ this sensitivity, awareness, and mindfulness to beneficial effect. Even if a cat has had a human companion, with whom they have been communicating for years, their communication and resulting relationship can always be further enhanced and improved.

§ § §

Remarkable Tales of Cats Who Whisper To Humans represents individual cats' own real-life experiences of using their cat Human-Whispering skills to move from homelessness to establishing a loving home with humans. As transcribed by Dr.Dayhoff, who is a cat whisperer, the following stories demonstrate how these cats employed their sharply honed abilities in selecting their human companions and specifically communicating with those humans. The result of successful cat

Human-Whispering is a mutually beneficial cat-human relationship in a permanent home with a lifetime of affection, care, fun, and respect.

§ § §

CHAPTER 3

FELIS

My name is "Felis." Or, more accurately, my name *was* Felis. According to my mother, whom I called "Mi-Mi-Ow," my brother, sister, and I hailed from ancient royalty called *Felidae*. Because of our lineage we have a Latin name and have specifically been catalogued by science as *Felis Silvestris Catus*. Ancient Egyptians considered us gods. Some Buddhists have believed that the souls of humans who attained a high degree of spirituality entered the bodies of cats.

That general reverence, however, has not continued to this day. Humans today seem to be less admiring of our heritage and inherent qualities. But, at least, they are not burning us alive or drowning us as witches as often as was once the general practice—although, cruelty and abuse still run rampant and occasionally are ritualized by research, medical schools, and mass shootings or poisonings. Gandhi railed against this—"The greatness of a nation and its moral progress can be judged by its treatment of animals." Mi-Mi-Ow was fond of his teachings though I do not know how she heard about him.

One might suspect the ancient Egyptians and Buddhists saw the special awareness or sensitivity that cats have always possessed with respect to humans. Mi-Mi-Ow impressed upon her kittens that this results from a highly-sharpened ability for observing and interpreting human behavior and responding appropriately without being fawning. Sounds like something human psychotherapists do from what I've heard. It was something not only of which to be proud but also by which to get on in the world and prosper.

I always tried to make Mi-Mi-Ow and my history proud. As a result, despite the domestic cat species, especially homeless and so-called "feral" cats, having fallen on difficult times, like royal human families during revolutions, cats have tended to always think of themselves as hailing from gentility. They epitomize being privy to and promoting the finer attitudes and appreciations of life. They are spiritually and psychically attuned to humans—perhaps through a sixth sense like Extra-Sensory Perception—in order to help humans help cats in a symbiotic relationship.

Like so many cats today, Mi-Mi-Ow missed out on the luxury of sleeping on a satin pillow by a sunny window or on a hearth of a blazing winter fire, all her needs being tended to, while being tempted with tasty Fancy Feast tidbits in a crystal goblet—if you can believe those TV commercials I have heard about. Instead, she had had the typical hard scrabble life of a homeless cat, living paw-to-mouth. When she gave birth to me, it was under an abandoned yellow Yugo in a rundown, weed-strewn strip mall parking lot. Only two of my siblings survived with me because Mi-Mi-Ow was so thin and worn out that she could not provide all her kittens with the nourishment we needed. She persevered, keeping us together and fed on mice until her inglorious end.

Having wandered into the field next to the squat concrete shopping area in search of dinner, she had been shot with BBs by several teenagers who had laughingly used her for target practice. She somehow dragged her bloodied body back to under the rusting car hulk where we were all gathered anticipating her return. Her death was slow and agonizing as she hung on to her last seconds of life. Desperately unwilling to let go, she tried not to show it, to spare us until the end.

Before she left us, she imparted more of Gandhi's teachings: "You must not lose faith in humanity. Humanity is an ocean; if a few drops of the ocean are dirty, the ocean does not become dirty." She explained that there were good humans out there who could and would help so we should seek them out. Still I wondered why humans were not as good as they should be in their capacity to empathize with others: *all* others. Mi-Mi-Ow also made us promise to always act in a manner befitting our high-born history and talent-elevated and spiritual status among animals. We mourned her passing quietly with dignity as we had promised her.

Despite my diminutive size, I always tried to hold my head high. When I was cleaned up, my long silky black whiskers, eyebrows, and fur brushed, I looked like a proper cat—a quite handsome, even elegant, gentleman cat. I could even daintily sip Earl Grey with pinkie claw up with catnip petit fours or scones, with clotted cream or lemon curd, at tea time and not look out of place. Indeed, no matter the situation, I tried, though not always successfully, to maintain my regal bearing.

The reason this had not always been possible was that I had spent my life constantly on the move, attempting to just survive as I followed my quest for what Mi-Mi-Ow referred to as the "Ultimate Purr"—the goal of all cats. What it was exactly she never said, only it had nothing to do with mating, having kittens, or endless access to fine food. It did have something to do with good humans. Supposedly I would know it when I found it.

As one might suppose, my life was filled with many "fur-raising" experiences along the way, the details of which I choose not to go into. I have no wish to indulge in a pity party here. However, it would not be telling tales out of school to say that there were many attempts by less-than-empathetic humans, dogs, raccoons, and cars to hurry my demise. At least someone had not, so far, tried to put an arrow through my head and display me as a photographed "trophy." Despite Mi-Mi-Ow's embrace of Gandhi, it has been hard to exist and manage in a world where so much violence, apathy, or just plain indifference is directed at you. It is as if you were a valueless object ... instead of being a flesh and blood creature sharing the Earth with humans, much less a revered feline knight in search of the Holy Grail of *Felis Silvestris Catus*.

If humans in general had had more awareness, sensitivity, and empathy for cats, and taken my plight to heart in the past, I would not have been in the state I was in when I hobbled into the yard of 51 Avon Road, in Wellesley, MA, on that balmy Spring

Saturday. Mare's tail clouds were scudding across the robin's-egg blue sky as the winds picked up aloft. Birds in the trees were chirping against a background hum of a propeller-driven aircraft high above, like the sound of a swarm of synchronous bees. It was a glorious day portending only good fortune.

My current indisposition forced me to hop-lope along as I made my way slowly into the yard. I had to travel up the inclined cement-block walkway along the right side of what was then a two-story red house with white shutters. Hugging the walkway, rows of multi-colored, crocus, snowbells, and grape hyacinth were fading as red tulips and vibrant yellow daffodils replaced them. For a moment I considered nibbling on the still-green, chlorophyll-laden, white-striped crocus leaves in the shade of the blooming dogwood. But I had more important business to conduct. I could always check them out later if necessary.

Alas, at that time I was not at my gentlemanly best. To my embarrassment my indisposition was obvious to all. It was not only that my once luxurious fur was anything but clean and brushed. But also it had become so tightly matted all over my body that it pulled and pinched my skin, causing significant pain with every tiny muscle movement. It felt like a tightly woven Berber carpet glued to every inch of me. Walking was torture, running well-nigh impossible. My overall appearance meant that my self-presentation this day was sadly inadequate to the task I had in mind. But the reality is that a cat cannot wait for "perfect" circumstances. As a general rule, "good enough" frequently has to be good enough.

While I was by nature a sterling example of an animal concerned about its appearance, in my travels around this heavily-treed bedroom suburb of Boston, I had had to pitch my kitty camp any place I could. This often included curling up under front porches where spiders and snakes resided. Here splinters from generations'-old wood caught and twisted my fur, holding me captive for hours, in danger of dog discovery. I had napped in dumpsters that reeked of tubs of green mold-covered cottage cheese, cadaver-smelling rotting meat scraps, and bagged doggy excrement. I had spent cold nights huddled in wheel wells of cars that had recently returned from the human's workplace.

I had also been caught for hours in the rain on asphalt-shingled shed roofs when raccoons looking for delicacies decided not to let me down unless I wanted to go paw-to-paw with them. While I believed in defending myself—every gentleman cat should know fisticuffs and at least one of the martial arts, I knew when I was out-numbered and out-weighed. But mostly I had hung out in privet bushes and native blackberry brambles that grew wild along untended property fence lines because they both shielded me and kept dogs and other antagonists at bay. However, they did not help my worsening fur-knotting situation any.

Because of the level of my skin discomfort I was going out of my way this crystal-clear afternoon to directly approach humans. My goal was primarily, hopefully, getting some tonsorial help. Or, at the very least, temporarily acquire some food. I knew my grotesquely matted hair would gain sympathy with people who did not hate cats: "Aww, you poor, poor kitty." But, at the same time, I was concerned that the condition of my muzzle would make them ill at ease. Despite how clean I tried to keep myself, somehow I had developed a disgusting-looking skin disorder which covered nearly all my face with tiny crusty sores. Only my eyes, nostrils, and ear tips were visible among the disease plaques. I could imagine humans being repelled, thinking I might be contagious or leprous, not wanting to touch me, much less help me.

There was no question that these sores itched mightily but I could no longer raise my back leg to scratch no matter how I twisted my aristocratic, anorexic-looking body. But even when I still had some flexibility to scratch, raking my claws over the sores only made them bleed in hot pain. Likewise, my carefully rubbing my face on the grass made the flaky lesions itch more ferociously.

In the maple treed yard ahead of me were two humans, one female and one male. They were on their knees pulling dandelions out of two large-sized patches of lawn and tossing them onto blue tarps. She was on an upper area, the backyard, and he, on a

14

lower, the side yard, separated by two stone steps. I made my way toward the male human because he was closer to me, though I would have preferred the female. I have found that females as a general rule tend to be more empathetic.

Sensuously I rubbed against his pant leg several times to get his attention. Looking into the human's eyes, I telegraphed him a smilingly friendly message of hello. Then casually—but very gently and uncomfortably—I slid over onto my back, exposing my matted belly. I knew if the male human had any affiliation with cats, he would likely resonate positively to my action. I had a sense he could not resist this blatant display of animal-to-animal communication. Exposing my belly and inviting the human to pet me there, I was showing him my heightened level of trust.

However, as embarrassing as it is to admit, the moment his big right hand descended to stroke my tangled fur, I panicked. I could not help myself. Fear engulfed me like a cold, black, suffocating blanket. Stunning recollections of incidents of human pretense at friendliness with their resulting unkindness flashed before me. Was that PTSD? I would not be surprised. Sometimes life seemed like a battle zone where you could not always be sure who the enemy was. Distrusting my positive instinct here, I immediately stiffened. On reflex I rolled forward onto myself. Automatically, I sank my teeth deeply into his hand. Like a tripped leg hold trap, exerting at least ninety pounds of pressure per square inch, I made a definite impression.

The moment I recovered from my dissociation, I was truly aghast. What had I done? It had not been my intention to harm the human. I had only been trying to get him into the mood to listen to my story, to help me. But the male human reared back on his knees, nearly falling over backward. Yelping, he gasped in shock as he attempted to right himself. His left hand grabbed his right which was dribbling blood from multiple dental punctures. Confusion and pain covered his face. His mouth hung open in disbelief.

When reality dawned on him, he called out to the female human, his voice strained, "I've, I've been ... bitten." She stood up, looking surprised, and leapt down the stone steps, racing toward him. He had straightened up and stood there, immobile. His hand was beginning to swell. His natural color was no longer present, replaced by a facial pallor that matched the nearby shutters. His hand simulated the house's barn red paint. His body began to sway.

"What happened?" she asked breathlessly as she looked at his ballooning appendage.

"The cat rolled over for me to pet him. When I tried to, he bit me."

The female human ran toward the back of the house. Quickly she returned with a dish towel to wrap around the male human's wound, a wallet, and two sets of keys. Without a word, she escorted him to their vehicle parked in the driveway. Bundling him into the passenger side, she backed up and peeled out. I hid under a privet bush by the front door, debating whether I dared to be there when they returned.

Prior to "the incident" as I preferred to think of it later, I had had the feeling—my antennae had told me—that this would likely be the end of my knight's quest. That is, it probably *would* have been had I not tenderized the male human's extremity with my incisors as efficiently as if I had employed a one-pound, studded, steel meat mallet. Now I needed to get through to them that I was indeed a gentleman cat, irrespective of what had happened, and they really, truly could trust me.

When they returned more than two hours later, the male human still looked ashen. Given his expression, it was hard to discern if he were trying to keep from fainting ... vomiting ... or both. His hand, which resembled Boston Red Sox Carlton Fisk's catcher's mitt, was immobilized in a dramatic-looking dressing and splint to limit its use and promote its elevation. I had a feeling that my bite probably had broken a bone as well. You know the horrific damage leg hold traps can do. Cradling his throbbing right hand as if it were a baby, he held his arm close to his chest and above his heart. The female human had a small amber vial gripped in her fist which likely meant he was on something strong for possible infection. At least I knew it was not rabies which raccoons and other wild creatures could carry but not I—not a gentleman cat.

As they walked to the front door, I heard them speak anxiously about something I knew had to do with me. That sounded serious. When she spied me still in the yard, her face did not confer feelings of endearment upon me. She pointed me out to the male human, who looked distracted, as if he wanted to bite a bullet or chugalug a fifth of vodka. I thought, Come on, gentlepeople, do I look like some ferocious wild beast who has come to maul or terrorize you? I am not Godzilla or the Cockroach That Ate Cincinnati.

The male human finally responded. But the female human shook her head to whatever he had said. She then looked over at me and for an instant I thought I detected a hint of empathy. She continued to watch me, noting I had not moved. I was trying to convey to her that I was friendly, contrary to our prior interaction. With an expression I could not interpret, she left him and started walking slowly toward me.

Since I could not be sure what she had in mind, I decided it was safer to leave. I heard somewhere, some time that "To withdraw isn't a sign of weakness ... It is a sign that a man [I am sure they meant a 'cat'] knows the limits of his capabilities and the most probable outcome of the future." I would come back later and try to communicate with her. Even with my mat-strapped legs, I managed to move more quickly—well, zig-zag more sharply—and reluctantly skittered into the next yard. She didn't chase or follow me. Muttering something, she turned back and they entered the house.

From under a prickly barberry just beyond the tall wooden, weathered picket fence separating the two properties, I watched warily. It was all so stupid. I had been so dumb and shamed Mi-Mi-Ow and my lineage. I had never bitten a human before. Why now when it was so important for me to make a good impression? Could I possibly get them to forgive me? Or had I inexorably wreaked all-out retaliation? I was deep in thought as night drew near. I disentangled myself from the barberry branches, crept back under the patinated boundary, and re-hunkered down in the privet near the front door.

It was important I not dwell on all my mistakes. Instead, I had to discover what I had learned from them. Aha! My plan was so super-simple *even* a dog could have thought of it—but not likely. Everything I did would be positive and relaxed. I would try hanging around their yard and not bite anyone again. I would show them how amiable I could be with my ears upright and my tail raised, well, raised as much as I could elevate it considering my challenging fur condition. Cocking my head to the side, I would try to communicate that the bite had been an accident ... that it would never happen again.

Apologizing was tough to do under the circumstances. Concentrating on my understanding of human emotional intelligence, perceptions, and body language, I would show them that I was not a threat. I respected them and they could respect me. I could be trusted. I would trust them in return. Moreover, I would be an ideal companion for them.

But what about their likely and understandable concern about my possibly having had rabies? As the days passed, I knew the male human would know he was not sick, despite his obviously thinking every muscle twitch or burp was predicting his hydrophobic death. Hopefully, rather than trying to capture me, he would monitor for actual symptoms and rationally wait out the disease incubation period, whatever that was.

According to cats which were better acquainted with the human approach to the disease than I, if any animal was "found to have rabies," the person bitten would have to receive rabies shots starting with rabies immune globulin, injected near the wound, to prevent the virus from infecting them. That would be followed by a series of four rabies vaccine injections in the arm over a period of fourteen days.

In the old protocol, the animal would already be dead—from the researcher killing it to test a portion of its brain for signs of the disease. Sadly, of all the animals killed for possible rabies, only six percent were actually found to be positive for the disease. That was not only inefficient and inhumane but also resulted unnecessarily in a lot of dead animals, including cats. There had to be a better way.

The good news was that in suburbia cats were a whole lot less likely to transmit rabies than wild animals. As analytical thinking replaced emotion in some public health issues, fortunately, more and more cats were being kept for a ten-day observation period, aka "quarantined," instead of instantly being slaughtered. Still, not a pleasant thought but better than the alternative. The cat grapevine could upon occasion be very enlightening.

Surprisingly, a few days after the "incident," the female human began putting out food every evening. While initially I was wary, my food-deprived gut urged me to take full advantage of the offering. Still I worried. Were these the type of humans who would try to poison me? I had already formed the impression that they were not, but I was basing that more on intuition than rational analysis. Despite my reluctance, I did finally indulge. It was good. I did not feel ill. Maybe that was a good sign.

At the same time I kept an eye open for either of them attempting to swoop down at me in the darkness, like the Wicked Witch of the West, to try to ensnare me as I ate. What came to mind were Mi-Mi-Ow's Two Essential Rules of Survival: (1) Always consider all the possible consequences and implications of any action ahead of time when dealing with humans. (2) Always have options available to deal with those consequences and implications. A cat could not be absolutely sure just what humans would try to do or why. But to put the odds in my favor, I continued telegraphing them: "You have been civilized so far. Let us continue to do this as civilized beings. No butterfly or fish catch nets, please."

During the day I hid in various places in their yard to watch for signs of human activity. When I spotted the female human, she spotted me. I threw my paws forward on the ground, well, as much as I was physically able to do. I lowered my head, raised my haunches, and glanced up at her as if ready to play. She came toward me. No longer seeing anger in her face or body, I did see both concern and eagerness. Since the emotions conflicted, I was not sure how to interpret them. Before she reached me, I looked into her eyes. I sent her a message. Something told me this was not yet the moment. It needed more work. I backed up to awkwardly limp off to the other property again.

Soon she started putting out small amounts of food both day and night. I was still not becoming ill—no vomiting or diarrhea or twitching—so I guessed it was okay. I never understood how anyone could poison animals given how sadistic it was. Their deaths were so agonizing. In my travels I chanced upon two Doberman pinchers lying by the side of the road. They had been poisoned. Their bodies were contorted, eyes wide open, and lips curled in a toothsome, sardonic grin of incredible pain. Strychnine did that.

Did someone do that on purpose or was that the result of poisoned bait put out to kill "nuisance" animals, like coyotes? Poisoned baiting was not only nasty but also stupid. Other animals would unknowingly feast on the poisoned carcasses. They too would be tortured and murdered. And for what: a simple, convenient, but knee-jerk "solution" to a perceived problem? Actions like that made me wonder about the ability of humans to rationally, critically, and compassionately solve problems.

The regularity of these small feedings was such a relief for my proto-starvation. Never before had I had the opportunity to languorously partake of any delicious cat and human food. In the back of my mind I worried about when it would stop. What would I do then? Go back to dumpster diving and begging? How humiliating. If only I were still regarded as royalty or the ultimate of spirituality, I could legitimately continue to expect to receive sustenance because it would have been seen as my due. More days passed and the snack delivery had not as yet slackened.

The next Saturday morning there was an old, slightly corroded Havahart trap stationed by the privet bush. In it the female human had placed a medium-size piece of raw chicken, the aroma of which wafted over to the fence where I was seeing to my elimination needs. It made me salivate. I brushed my right paw over my mouth to wipe away the drool before I headed back to the scene of the crime.

Leading up to the cage door like a trail of bread crumbs were tiny pieces of the breast meat. My olfactory nerves mesmerized, I entered the yard and dream-walked to the privet bush. Of course, despite the hypnotic spell I was under, my sixth sense was operating, making me ever-alert to my environment. If necessary, it would direct me to hide. But no humans appeared to be present—not at the door or at the windows. Cautiously I nibbled the tiny morsels one by one as they wound their way to the cage: it was the feline version of "Hansel and Gretel."

In my state of still-unrequited hunger, I had an important decision to make. Did I want to risk entering the trap? Had I gotten through to the female human? Was I misjudging her body language which suggested empathy? I was no novice at assessing potentially dangerous situations. I knew if I had misjudged the female human, it could be very bad, perhaps even lethal, for me. However, I felt—maybe wanted to believe—the two humans had not only received but also appropriately interpreted all the positive messages I had repeatedly sent them. At this point, I had to let my intuition dictate my actions.

After I let the last miniscule chicken morsel slither down my gullet, I rubbed my side against the cage. Holding my breath, I thought of Mi-Mi-Ow and her quoting Gandhi, "Strength doesn't come from physical capacity. It comes from an indomitable will." Okay, Mi-Mi-Ow, I hope you are right. I stepped inside. From experience I knew nothing would happen until the door spring was released.

The door spring was attached to the metal plate which was lying flat in the rear of the cage. I could smell the 3-in-1 oil which had been used to lubricate the connections. On the metal plate the chunk of raw chicken sat, tantalizingly beckoning me. All right, I thought, I have come this far. I have to take the chance things will work out in my favor. I have read and analyzed the signs. I have done what I could. Now I have to trust my Human-Whispering.

I inched forward, letting my tongue graze the fresh white meat. My taste buds were standing erect. The aroma was heady. It blended with the fragrance of the white and orange narcissus near the privet, oddly enhancing its seductiveness. The crumbs leading up to the trap had only whetted my appetite, like shrimp cocktail before the filet mignon entrée. I continued to lick, trying not to shift the non-poisonous bait's position on the platform just yet.

Why had I been hesitating? A dust mote of doubt gripped me. That was annoying. I had already decided. Internally shaking my head, I pawed the flesh. Its soft moistness yielded to my touch. Swooning with images of gustatory nirvana, I took the plunge. I grabbed that hunk of chicken. Snap. The platform, now free of the weight, lifted smoothly, and slammed the cage door shut. The noise startled me even though I had been expecting it. I let my arousal subside then focused on devouring my kitty feast.

Okay, it is your turn now, humans, I thought, my heart beating faster than normal. I let you "trap" me. Do not disappoint me. Rescue me. I could hear myself almost pleading. Come on, Felis, I chastised myself. Do not be so undignified. You are of the royal family. At least act with decorum.

The front door on the side of the house opened with a swooshing sound as the rubber weather stripping released its hold on the door sill. The two humans peered out at me. As they talked between themselves, I tried my best to appear calm, hoping to further reinforce the notion that I was just a homeless feline who wanted and needed a loving home. I trusted they would compassionately provide it to me.

I do not know what I expected to happen next, but what did happen astonished me. The female human walked out, down the steps, and picked up the trap. Looking as if she were examining me, she smiled. I lifted my whiskers in return. Carefully she carried the trap and me to the car and placed it onto the passenger seat. She wrapped seatbelt around the trap. It felt claustrophobic but seemed like a good human sign. Unsure what it all meant, I tried to relax and think positively, transmitting those thoughts to her accompanied by a lilting meow or two. Even cats know the William Congreve quotation, "Music hath charms to sooth the savage breast."

In fifteen minutes we were in a sterile-looking, white-walled room with lots of other humans and animals. At least it was not a research laboratory. Nervous cats sitting in expensive carriers or wearing harnesses with leashes sitting on human laps looked askance at me. I could hear them, their telepathic inquiries drifting my way, "How did you let yourself get caught in that contraption? You're a cat. You're smarter than that." I just lifted my whiskers and nodded as I chuckled to myself, Yes, I should certainly hope so. We'll see.

Of course, it was a veterinary clinic. I had never been to one before but certainly had heard about them. Why was I here? Suddenly it came to me. Of course. Many days had elapsed since the bite. Neither the male human nor I had shown any obvious signs of illness. Neither of us had a headache, fever, vomiting, irritability, excessive movements or agitation, confusion, hallucinations, aggressiveness, bizarre or abnormal thoughts, or muscle spasms. The rabies incubation period had passed. Good news: we both were okay. No surprise here.

Hey, gentlepeople, I had tried repeatedly to tell you this. I may have been an aesthetic mess but I was not ill. I had no symptoms. My skin condition, while repulsive, did not bespeak of rabies. Apparently neither one of them had really listened to me. But, maybe, as was often typical of humans, they were too caught up in the emotional import of the moment to be mindful of anything else. According to Alexander Pope, "To err is human." I forgave them so you know what it says about the acknowledged spiritually-elevated status of cats.

As we sat there among many varieties of my species, waiting, I began to contemplate all that had happened. "Why" shouted for an answer. Why had she caught me? Why had she brought me here? What did it mean for afterward? While I had done the terrible deed, was her only purpose in trying to catch me due to her concern about possible rabies in her male human? Did she care about me at all?

With all my heart I had wanted her actions to be less purely practical and more complimentary and caring than that. I wanted to believe that once she saw my friendly behaviors and heard my messages, she would see me in a whole new, positive light and in context. I was not just as a cat who had harmed someone out of fear and panic. I was a cat who was seeking a warm, loving, and mutually beneficial relationship. I was a cat who would enhance her life.

She smiled at me again. Her whole face contributed to the smile, from her upturned lips to her dimpled cheeks to her crinkling eyes. I could feel the warmth of that smile. It was like being caressed in swirling, incandescent gold flecked light. Her thoughts told me clearly I had gotten through to her. My "whys" disappeared so I could concentrate on what was ahead of me here and now.

When she was called in to a small room with a cold metal table, a male human in white, stethoscope draped around his neck—no doubt the veterinarian—carefully removed me from the trap, and began fondling me. Fondling? Gentlemen cats are not fondled. Well, perhaps that was too harsh an assessment of his actions. Let us just say he was not petting me. He was poking, prodding, then oops! Excuse me! I had not expected a thermometer, even coated in Vasoline, to invade my private parts! That seemed quite unnecessary and certainly disrespectful. However, I chose to take it in stride with a Zen-like demeanor in keeping with my gentle, regal disposition.

Following his manual exam, the vet shaved a spot on my neck and stuck in a needle to withdraw blood. Not yet finished with needles, he injected vaccines under the skin in a spot triangulated by my shoulder blades. Then he induced me—that is a polite way of saying he held open my jaw and threw a small pill toward the back of my mouth—to swallow a sedative. It made me drowsy and wobbly quickly so I did not have much time to consider how discourteous his actions were. It turned out that pill was to allow him to proceed to carefully remove my mats without slicing-and-dicing me. The eventual denuding of my patrician body took some time, further adding to my royal embarrassment. Fortunately he somehow managed not to nick my skin ... well, not to the point of gushing blood anyway.

Next a technician carried me to a metal sink with a sprayer for a bath. Having been responsible for my own cleanliness since Mi-Mi-Ow left, I felt it was highly insulting for them to take such liberties. It took two of them to hold me so I would not submerge in the water or panic. I had no intention of panicking, thank you. But etiquette demanded they ask my permission before embarking on manhandling me or trying to "drown" me.

Before everyone who participated in this major theatrical production number was done, the veterinarian had scraped some of the lesions on my face. Sir, you could have frozen the skin first. That hurt. Examining the tissue under a microscope, he told the female human I had folliculitis, an infection of the hair follicles. For it he gave her four weeks of nasty-tasting antibiotics for me to ingest. Did that mean putting up with more jaw clamping and pill thrusting? I beg your pardon. How unsuitable. In the meantime, I remained controlled and insouciant. There was neither a hiss nor a growl emanating from my demure person. It was still important that I appear to be the friendliest, most tolerant of cats, one that would never bite anyone even if sorely provoked, which, unbeknownst to them, I surely was.

With me on a hand towel in the Havahart back on the front seat of the car, I talked non-stop all the way back to the house. Conversing with the female human about cats and life in general, I saw she was listening to me. She even added to the conversation with free and easy-sounding responses. This reinforced the notion that I was not about to be seduced and abandoned. If the truth be told, being clean and mat-free (also known as "naked"), I felt like a new cat, one actually able to soon saunter, trot, and gallop again. Soon my skin would stop hurting and itching. Soon I would have my gorgeous coat back. Ah, freedom was mine!

Back at the house, the female human immediately carried me into the house Carefully removing me from the trap, speaking softly all the while, she then placed me in a ten-by-twelve-sq.ft room all by myself. It had a single bed that looked soft. On the carpet were several layers of newspaper on which were dishes of water and dry food, a litter pan, and a cat-sized foam bed. It was obvious that the male human, knowing what the female human had in mind, had set it up in our absence. That was reassuring.

From that moment on they visited with me, talking to me, seemingly listening. They tested to see how close I would let them come. The male human did seem a bit tentative at first about trying to touch me. I guess the thought of another throbbing catcher's mitt made him particularly reluctant. No problem. No need to worry about recurring punctures. I was on my very best behavior.

Not requiring a whole lot of coaxing, I was more than ready to take my proper place in this household. When I let them touch and stroke me, I began to see what Mi-Mi-Ow had meant by the "Ultimate Purr." In a matter of two days I had "persuaded" the humans to let me meet the two other house felines. Of course, I made sure I displayed only politeness, patience, and tolerance, as was required of royalty—you know, *noblesse oblige*. Then, without an invitation, I simply took it upon myself to explore the entire house. They seemed pleased with my initiative and enthusiasm.

I settled in and became part of the family. Quickly I included in that lap and bed privileges. Over time the male human's hand finally healed and we bonded ... big time. Thereafter, he spent a lot of time rubbing and brushing my aristocratic tummy as I writhed on his lap purring loudly. I also curled around his head on his pillow at night. I was still working on trying to convince them that they should call me "Felis." Unfortunately, Human-Whispering does not guarantee that a cat can get humans to dot every "i" and cross every "t" precisely as a cat wants. Humans can be bright but, alas, not as bright as cats. However, it was more than enough that my Human-Whispering had guaranteed me my loving home with those who listened and truly cared.

§ § §

CHAPTER 4

KITSY

It was around noon on a late spring day. A few clouds littered the bright blue sky like solitary dollops of whipped cream. Cherry and plum trees were showing off their soft pink blossoms. Red and yellow parrot tulips, yellow daffodils, and purple hyacinth were popping through the softened dark soil. They dotted the earth with an embarrassment of color. Grass sprigs were making their comeback appearance among the stiff brown tufts of grass of winter that covered all the front and back yards.

It was these sorts of warmer days that made me happy as I made my daily walk around my neighborhoods. I'm a three-year-old, thirteen-pound, domestic short-haired black cat who has had to spend his life wandering. Nearly the size of a Jack Russell, I had developed a slight football shape that has seemed to be unimpressive to those enamored with the cat species.

My territory—the area I defend—was comprised of four long through streets and two dead ends. They all joined the main thoroughfare, Rockland, less than a half-mile from town. My territory would have been much larger except for the herds of vicious dogs that frequently rampaged through the area. These savage beasts kept the animal control officers busy chasing them. They put children and smaller animals, such as squirrels, chipmunks, rabbits, quail, small dogs and puppies, and cats in fear for their lives. They had even killed a small herd of adult llamas, as well as their babies, that had provided cart rides for children and wool for weaving at a farm at the edge of town. Somehow they had scaled the seven-foot cyclone fence that surrounded the llamas' barn and paddock and had gratuitously ripped out the animals' throats.

Despite my size, I was tough. I also knew when to pick my battles—something most cats learned fast or didn't survive. One dog I might be able to manage with four sets of long needle-point claws sunk in to the canine's back or jowls, but dealing with a canine tag team made it all unsportsmanlike and potentially lethal. I never understood how dogs could fight until they were bloodied, missing parts of their bodies, and near death's door. My apologies to human dog aficionados, but from my experience dogs aren't very bright.

As one might expect, life on the street has been hard. I'd seen humans look at me astonished by my battered condition and that I'd lived this long given it. Sadly too often they didn't do anything to help me continue to live. It was humans that had originally wrenched me from my mother while I was still suckling then tossed me into a dumpster like a dirty tissue.

I was too young to understand what had happened then or why. All I knew was that this new location was cold, damp, dark, and reeking with all kinds of un-catlike smells. Still uncoordinated, I had struggled to climb over the sharp and slippery contents to find my mother. I knew she was waiting for me, somewhere. Wherever she was, I knew she was in a dry comfortable place, poised to cuddle with me and feed me. But no matter where I looked I couldn't find her. I don't know whether I was more confused or scared as a result.

Now having missed several meals, I was so hungry my stomach hurt. What was I supposed to do? Having seen my mother lick food, I tried my paw at licking whatever I could find. Even though everything tasted bad, I tried to get it down. Soon I was vomiting and had diarrhea. That made the pain worse. Time passed as I shivered. I curled up in my own waste for warmth.

Desperate, I cried piteously for my mother. The more I cried, the more my already small voice lost its force. I had to stop intermittently because it wasn't long before only a baby-bird chirp sound came out. The cold damp and my hunger were sapping my strength. My body temperature which my mother had regulated before was beginning to drop. Feeling very sleepy, I would intermittently drop off, awaken, and then drop off again. I had no way of knowing how long I had been in this kitten purgatory.

When I aroused myself one more time, I made my last attempt to utter any sound that might gain my mother's attention. I knew she was searching for me, bereft at my loss. But I heard nothing back. As I dropped off again, the ear-shattering grinding of metal on metal stabbed me broad awake. Above me I could see the heavy lid of the refuse container rising slowly into the air. The light blinded me. As my eyes began to adjust a little, I could barely make out the shadowy form of a human. Oh no! It was intently scanning the contents of the dumpster. Was it looking for me? It seemed to be specifically looking for something.

My heart was galloping, making my whole body heave. I tried to make myself as inconspicuous as possible amid the banana peels and Styrofoam peanuts. It was humans who had stolen me from my mother and tossed me in here, laughing. Next I heard a gasp come from the human form. It was now staring directly at me. I had to make a stand. My eyes wide, I attempted to raise my fur and tail on end and growl like an adult, to frighten and dissuade the human. But all I could emit was the low, rough sound of a microscopic buzz saw. I was going to die. Mama!

Speaking to me softly, a female human voice said, "Oh, there you are. I thought I heard something. You poor, poor little thing. Oh my God! Who did this to you? Whoever it was should rot in hell. Okay, kiddo. We have to get you out of here and warmed up as soon as possible. And I'll bet some food wouldn't hurt."

I was stunned. What was going on? She didn't sound like the humans who had callously chucked me into the dumpster. Should I attack her anyway, just to make sure? As she spoke, she opened a sack-like handbag and pulled out a red acrylic baby blanket. She reached into the receptacle and gently extricated my shivering body from the waves of diarrhea-covered garbage lapping at my sides. The next thing I knew I was enveloped in the fuzzy fabric. She opened her L.L. Bean Thinsulate-lined coat and held me against her chest, wrapping me inside it. The warmth felt good. The loud thump, thump, thump resonating within her chest reminded me of my mother before I was born and later when we snuggled. I missed her terribly. Maybe this was good. Maybe this human would be different, I hoped. Maybe she wouldn't hurt me. Maybe I'll be back with my mother again soon. Maybe.

After my rescue, I did a lot of sleeping on a heating pad set to "low." The female human, named "Fran," gave me kitten formula through what looked like a doll's baby bottle at pre-determined times throughout the following days and nights. My tummy soon began to look almost bulbous by comparison. When I was placed on a human's blanket on the floor after a few days, I managed to walk around, mostly without falling over. Now that I was feeling better, there was so much to see and do. I wanted to explore and discover.

But I still hadn't found my mother. Instead Fran acted like my mother, nuzzling me and cleaning up after me. It was Fran who ferried me to a veterinarian to check me out for viruses, parasites, and diseases. Despite my previously unhygienic surroundings and questionable diet in the dumpster, I received a tentative "all clear" from the vet. She was told I was very lucky to have survived.

I can't express how much I still missed my mother. Being away from her had left a gaping hole in me. And yet, the months that followed with Fran were like kitty heaven by comparison with my stint in the alley trash. I had all my basic needs met as well as lots of play and petting.

As it turned out, Fran was a cat rescuer who checked alleys for stray cats. In that role she knew to check out trash receptacles of all kinds where cruel people often abandoned live, abused, and neglected cats, letting them die slow, torturous deaths. She volunteered with an all-volunteer, non-profit, no-kill shelter. After fostering ten kittens she had rescued from a hoarder, she finally adopted them. Now there were ten adults occupying her small apartment. She could barely handle the cats she had without adding me to the fold as other than a kitten. Unfortunately, there appeared to be no other volunteer available to foster a wee one like me.

Her fostering a kitten meant that once I was old enough, I would have to go to the companion animal shelter's adoption clinics on weekends—on both Saturday and Sunday. These were located at a large, well-known local pet emporium. The cats up for adoption had their two tiers of cages staged on long conference tables in the front of the store, near the shaded plate glass window. This caught the eye of potential human companions. There the cats' playful antics drew adopters-to-be into the adoption area.

By this time I was morphing into a sleek, handsome, sweet-natured youngster. So every weekend Fran and I traveled to and from adoption clinic. But very soon it became a boring and frustrating ritual. Lots of humans, large and small, stared at me, poked fingers at me though the cage bars, and said stupid things to me. An occasional wet dog snout intruded into my cage. It stressed me out, leaving me conflicted about whether to retreat to the back of the cage or pierce his nostrils for diamond studs. That retaliation, however, would not have made me popular among potential adopters or the stupid dog owners who had thoughtlessly let their canine invade my captive space. When you're in a cage, you can't run and you can't hide.

This would be my routine until I was adopted. The rescue group's leader, Harriet, named me "Kitsy," after a small black rescue dog she had had as a child. However, potential adopters were constantly chuckling about my name as they passed by. "Kitsy? As in kitsy-kitsy-koo?" Dumb. At least they could get it right: it's "kitchy-kitchy-koo." Those reactions didn't signal warmth toward me.

As a baby, I had had luxurious fur but things were changing. My eventual football-shape was apparently beginning to be obvious. Irrespective of my shape, because I was continually not being chosen for adoption I was rapidly becoming an adolescent. Adolescent cats were not as in demand as kittens. No, it was kittens that were almost always being adopted immediately. Soft, cute, and helpless, they were always more popular than the adolescent I was quickly becoming at four months of age.

As a result, it was my cage mates that were cuddled, petted, and oohed and ahhed over. I had no idea why so many people seemed to ignore me. I was friendly and fun loving. I showed my playful side whenever people drew near. I reached out my paw, with claws retracted, to them through the cage bars. I rubbed my face against their fingers. I was sending positive affirmations to them with everything I had. But it still didn't seem to help. It occurred to me that maybe they wanted a less playful or outgoing cat. Did that make sense? I just didn't know. How could I know? But trying to look less active didn't help either.

Something finally dawned on me as I monitored other young cats being adopted. Those cats were in many colors but rarely all black like me. Maybe it was my color. Yes, even with the little kittens, it seemed that the black ones were the last to be adopted if they were adopted at all. Fran too was becoming depressed about my seeming "un-adoptability."

She walked over to my cage on a Saturday afternoon and said, "Sweetie, I'm sorry that you keep being left behind. It's not about you. You're a wonderful cat. But people tend not to want to adopt a black cat. I don't know if they're being superstitious. But the combination of you being older and black seems to be the kiss of death for your adoption. I wish I had the space for another permanent cat, especially one like you, because I'd adopt you in an instant. I just don't have the room while I continue to temporarily take in kittens in need." She looked forlornly into my eyes. I looked back and begged her not to abandon me, to figure out something. I didn't think I could take being discarded again.

But then, something happened. It seemed that somehow there was a possibility of me having a forever home with someone other than Fran. A couple came by late on Saturday. They actually looked at me, handled and tentatively petted me. They didn't reject me outright. Things were looking up. Maybe I could break out in my kitty "happy dance." All the other kittens around me had been adopted into loving homes. And now ... and now ... it looked as if I just might be taken to my own as well. I felt a glow of anticipation.

I looked around for Fran to share my happiness. She, however, was taking a few minutes to shop for dry and canned food for her permanent cats and formula for her kitten fosters. And Harriet, the rescue group's leader, was gone too, delivering two adopted cats and not scheduled to return for another twenty minutes. That left a volunteer named Judy to handle the possible adoption.

However, what I didn't know would have given me immediate significant pause. My human parents-to-be were deep in a serious discussion with Judy. As I strained to listen, I heard and felt the negativity of what they were saying. Something was very wrong. If I could have translated it all accurately, I would have rocked my cage to tumble it to the floor to frighten them off.

"Is this all you have? It's not exactly what we were looking for. We were looking for a real kitten."

"We are always getting more kittens in but there's no guarantee when that will be. This is a very nice cat. He's just a little older than the other kittens we've had lately."

"Yeah, well, we were looking for a small ball of fluff we could play and cuddle with. We thought that would be fun. You know, something that liked to be petted and wasn't much trouble. Not something that has started its adult behaviors. He doesn't look like a baby anymore."

Judy's face dropped as her concern about their attitude about having a cat increased. "Kittens are a lot of trouble because they are babies and need lots of close monitoring and care. And they grow very fast into cats so it doesn't take long before they outgrow that tiny, super-cute stage. Soon you will have an adult cat who will live with you on average for thirteen years. Perhaps this cat is not really what you want."

I looked around for Fran. She wasn't back yet. I moved from side to side in my cage, hoping my movement would concern them. They either ignored me or didn't notice.

The couple, who said their names were Jack and Betty, looked annoyed. They argued heatedly with Judy, "We're going to take that cat. It's as close as we're going to get to a kitten, I guess. If he's well-behaved, everything should work out all right."

Judy blanched. "It's important you know that he's still a youngster so he hasn't learned what he needs to know about living with humans. They have to learn to be 'well-behaved.' It will take time, kindness, and direction. They don't know this automatically. You may not know much about cats yet. But cats, small or big, act like cats." Betty was grimacing and Jack was rolling his eyes.

Judy continued in earnest, "Each one has a different personality, but they all have similar cat behaviors. They have to learn through positive reinforcement and lots of love what they are allowed and not allowed to do in your home. I mean, until they learn, they are likely to do what kittens and cats do, that is make what we consider 'mistakes.' Perhaps you might want to learn a little about more cat behavior before adopting one so you know what to expect."

They slowly shook their heads, looking insulted by the suggestion. "Don't tell us what we know or don't know or what we should do."

"I'm merely suggesting that cat behavior isn't necessarily what a person who doesn't know cats expects or wants. You and the cat will have to work out a mutually-beneficial relationship, as you would with another human being. In many ways having a pet is like having a young child."

I could see their facial expressions made Judy uncomfortable. "Oh, for God's sake!" they both responded in exasperation, "It's *just* an animal. We're not adopting a child!"

"But you are adopting a child!" Judy was getting angry and defensive. Their tone, volume, and body language were freaking me out. Where is Fran? When is she coming back? Fran would stop this insanity ASAP if Judy didn't. I wanted to call for Fran but was afraid to. While my yowling might stop Jack and Betty, I didn't know what other consequences there might be.

Judy seemed to think that they didn't understand what they were getting themselves into and really needed to know. That it was up to her to educate them. They didn't seem to understand that a cat was not a play toy to be available for their fun then to be put aside on a shelf when they were finished, until the next time. They seemed to be oblivious to the fact that a cat was a thinking, feeling, living being, a member of the family with its own wants and needs, and not an object.

Conflict overwhelmed Judy. It was obvious she hated being in this position. She looked around for Fran or Harriet. I was sending her messages: Don't let them take me! Fran and Harriet were nowhere in sight. This couple was demanding to adopt me right then and there but Judy didn't want to let them. She did NOT have to. All she had to do was say, "NO!" After all, they couldn't simply take me.

But she bit her lower lip as if to say, If only Fran or Harriet were here. They'd know how to handle this. They'd tell them "No, no way." Either one would explain that it was the group's responsibility to match people with cats and adopt only to people who wanted the cat to be treated as a "family member." But neither was there to do the right thing.

I could see Judy felt intimidated as she seemed to slouch onto herself and look at the floor. She not only hated disagreements but also found asserting herself nearly impossible. Wanting to shout at them and dig in her heels, she knew she could not stand up to these strong people for long. For everything she said they had an argument. It didn't matter that Judy was the one with the power to grant or prevent the adoption. If only she had thought of it, she could have feigned an "asthma attack" or even a "seizure" to forestall having to deal with them further, giving time for Fran to return. But she ultimately acceded to Jack and Betty who filled out the paperwork and provided their adoption check. I had to stop this but what could I do? What should I do?

I wondered if I wriggled out of their grip, hissed, growled, or scratched them, if they would let go and forget about me. But I was afraid I'd be automatically labeled an "aggressive" or "problem" cat. No one would or could know what had precipitated my negative behavior. They wouldn't know about my motivation and intent, that I was justified. They would simply assign it as part of my personality. I might be sent to the city pound where I'd be euthanized for sure.

I had to stop this but what could I do? What should I do? At the very least, it was likely to make me even less adoptable than I already was. Was that even possible? Harriet and Fran wouldn't know about Judy's not wanting to adopt me to them—she certainly wasn't going to tell them and risk their wrath. I could see she felt bad enough about it and herself already. I was caught in a web not of my making. The question was: Was it really as bad as it seemed? If so, could I survive it?

Judy pointed out several times that in signing the adoption papers they were *promising* to return me to the rescue group and get their money back if things didn't work out with me. I had seen some cats come back after leaving with adopters. At this point I was torn between my previous joy of finally being adopted and my being adopted by these two angry humans who didn't seem to care about me one bit. If I couldn't stop it, what could I do to calm the waters?

The happy future to which I had looked forward with hope was not meant to be. My new "parents" quickly revealed in spades they had never had a cat before. Neither one had ever had *any* kind of animal companion before, even as children. They were only-children who were the center of adult attention and pretty much got what they wanted from their parents and others.

They couldn't seem to relate to me. All they really knew about cats was that you didn't need to walk them. Cats could amuse themselves. Cats were self-sufficient and needed only the most basic of care. Cats would be there always available for the humans "they idolized," their adopters. They seemed to like the idea of being looked up to as gods, provided with fitting adulation, and always strictly obeyed.

As a result, Jack and Betty expected me to be a perfect, little furry, no-problem, non-companion "companion." That meant I was expected to be neat in my cat pan and never let my litter smell. I would never meow loudly or interrupt them on the phone, when they were eating, with guests, or watching television. I would never get on the bed or wake them up in the morning. I would never play when they didn't want to. I would always accept their playing and petting no matter how I felt: sick or well, happy or sad or angry. I would treat them as if the sun rose and set on them.

Furthermore, I would never show my claws or teeth, growl or hiss. I would never cough up a hairball on the wooden floor, carpet, or furniture. I would not shed my fur on clothing, the furniture, carpeting, or throw rugs. I would not climb onto shelves, counters, the refrigerator, or go into the closets. In other words, I was not to be a "cat." With their unrealistic expectations of me as a "pet," I was bound to do everything wrong ... which, sadly, I did.

The afternoon the day after my adoption they saw me scratch their newly-purchased upholstered chair. They both freaked out. "What the—?" They were furious, waving their arms. Both of them screamed at me, "Stop it! You stupid, miserable excuse for a pet!" Then shaking their heads as if I were justifying all their negative expectations, Betty added, "What can you expect. I knew you were trouble the moment we first spotted you!" They tried to hit me with a fly swatter as they continued shouting, "You ever scratch the furniture again and it's curtains for you, buster! Stupid, crummy cat!"

As confused and scared as I had been in the dumpster, I now was petrified. I hid under the tan leather and teak sofa in the living room and stayed there for days. That was partly because whenever they walked by the sofa, where they knew I was hiding, they said unpleasant things in an angry tone. It was obvious they meant it for me. As a result, I came out only when no one was around. It was only at those moments that I ate, drank, or used the litter pan. At least they had still left out dry food for me. But I didn't know for how long that would be. The timing of my venturing out from under the sofa meant I would and did have unintentional accidents under that piece of furniture. I didn't mean to but I didn't dare leave my secure place to use the litter pan when they were nearby.

My human companions didn't seem to understand me, much less respect me. They thought like humans and nothing else seeped through. They couldn't—or wouldn't?—interpret the messages I sent them no matter how hard I tried. They couldn't seem to put themselves in my place, to understand why I seemed to them to be such a "hostile, oppositional cat." I was afraid of their anger and the potential accompanying pain.

Everything they said and did seemed full or rage and violence. Yet they indicated they couldn't understand why *I* seemed to *purposely* do things to annoy them. In only a matter of a couple of days they had determined there was nothing fun about having me around. They shouted at me to "Come here" or "Go away." I was an increasingly merely a large irritation to them.

They acted as if I had been that small ball of fluff-like kitten they had really wanted, I wouldn't have scratched their chair and created this problem. It never seemed to have occurred to them that if I had been a small kitten, I would still likely have scratched the furniture. Moreover, if I had had a scratching post that Judy recommended, I might never have considered scratching the chair. But this was the Twilight Zone.

It was *my* fault that they had chosen not to spend the money on a carpet-covered wood form which I could legitimately and naturally scratch. Even though my new companions had the money to expend on one, they stressed it was an unnecessary expense despite Judy's urging. After they *had* to buy *all* my cat essentials—bowls, food, litter pan, litter, harness, leash, and carrier—they said they weren't interested in spending anything more on me. I was "only an animal."

Because they knew nothing about cats, they seemed to think that I didn't need to stretch and sharpen my claws so I could be ready to catch my dinner if necessary. They didn't seem to think that as I grew older, I needed to practice being an adult cat. I wasn't going to be a kitten forever. No, I was there to provide them with entertainment, something they could switch on and off, period.

That meant it was not up to them to help me develop my behavior. I wasn't a "child" though Judy ridiculously thought so. They didn't want to have to show and teach me what was scratchable and what was not. They didn't bargain on being teachers and having to remind me repeatedly when I made mistakes. I wasn't supposed to make mistakes in the first place. Fran taught me things and never once yelled at me when I erred. She corrected my unacceptable behavior gently and quickly, redirected my attention, and rewarded my correct behavior. But Jack and Betty weren't Fran.

As was all too clear, their attitudes about me and their expectations of me never gave the relationship the chance to work out. Furthermore, my hiding from Jack and Betty made them even angrier. They would shout at me to come out. They would kick the sofa leg as they went by. The noise and movement suggested that it still wasn't safe to check things out when they were around. They wanted me out but they were angry with me when I was out. I was damned either way. What was I to do? It was only after they went to bed each evening that I could safely eat, drink, eliminate, and stretch my legs.

It seemed that nothing I did pleased them. When I did not greet their return at the kitchen door, instead running back under the sofa, they were miffed. They grumbled, "Wasn't part of having a pet its greeting you happily when you returned?" I couldn't. I was too busy cowering, afraid they might just kill me for something else. Impatiently they called me to come. Despite how they tried to disguise it, their angry body language and tone of voice kept my body shaking constantly when they were around. This went on for five days.

Finally, Jack and Betty made it obvious they had had it with this "disappointing, no-good cat." They had no intention of continuing to put up with an animal that didn't obey them. I was no fun. I wasn't playful. I didn't show them respect. I didn't show them I was glad to see them. I wasn't a little ball of fur they could cuddle. Because I stayed in hiding, I hadn't even allowed them to pet me after I scratched the chair. I didn't show the automatic love and trust they expected from a pet. As I heard them repeatedly rant, "No animal has the right to treat us that way." They affirmed they were simply not going to put up with it any longer.

So none too carefully, they tried jabbing and pushing me out from under the sofa with a broom. The spines stung my back, legs, and belly. It hurt. They nearly caught me in the face with one poke. Not my eyes! I kept backing away toward the rear of the sofa. When I saw them stare at me, trying to reach my location under the sofa, the look on their faces was malevolent. I was so frightened I didn't know what to do. Feeling it was safer to stay where I was, quivering, I didn't budge.

As they looked under the sofa, they discovered to their shock that I had had the audacity—the unmitigated gall—to have had several bowel movements under there. They went ballistic. "You disgusting creature. How dare you poop under our Danish Modern sofa. And on our nice clean carpet! That is so gross! We gave you a litter pan to use. And how do you repay us for it? By doing this? You ungrateful wretch! I won't have a un-house-broken animal in my house. Do you hear me?! You don't deserve to call our home yours."

Going all out, they both grabbed at me to forcibly drag me out. While trying to avoid my accidents, they found their arms wouldn't reach me as I lay paralyzed against the wall. "Oh, yeah! I've got news for you, buddy!" called Jack as they moved the sofa from the wall.

Unceremoniously, they hauled me out, holding me roughly by the scruff of my neck. Jack spanked me hard across my haunches. The repeated blows to my lower body hurt terribly. And then, to make matters worse, my bladder, which I had been holding all this time, unintentionally gave way. I couldn't help myself. I began to urinate on the floor. Now in full panic mode, I started growling and hissing. Unsuccessfully I swiped at Jack's arm with my sharp, unclipped kitten claws. I was trying anything I could to make him stop.

However, showing my pain, fear, and anger did nothing to stop him. If possible, it made Jack angrier with me than I could have imagined. Betty and Jack both shouted, "How dare you try to scratch us, you vile creature! Look what you just did on the carpet! You filthy, miserable excuse for a pet. We did you a big goddamn favor by adopting you! And this is how you return the favor?! We never ever want to see you again."

Jack shook my body vigorously. My whole body screamed in pain. I looked at them with eyes wide and pupils dilated as if to beg: No more. Don't hurt me any longer. Please stop. What do I have to do to make you stop? I'll do anything. But they didn't stop. Before I knew it, Betty had yanked open the front door and Jack had hurled me out into a snow bank. The front door slammed door behind me with a resounding thud.

Covered in white, wet crystals, I shook myself very gently. My body ached all over. Fortunately, the fall hadn't further injured me as far as I could tell. My landing had been cushioned by several feet of snow which had drifted against the country-styled stone wall out front. Had the snow not been there, it would have been a totally different story. I probably would have died instantly or been so badly injured I would have died in excruciating pain some time thereafter.

Dislodging myself from the snow drift, I looked longingly at the front door. I didn't understand all that had transpired. Despite their angry behavior and words at the adoption clinic, once they had adopted me, I wanted the situation to work out. I tried to hold up my kitten end of the bargain as I understood it. And still, even after all that had happened, part of me was *almost* willing to try again—almost, but not quite. In point of fact, I was too terrified of them to try to figure out what exactly it was they wanted of me.

While cats are highly intelligent, they can't resolve problems with humans all by themselves. It didn't take a human to figure that one out. Cat-human problems are always a matter of one's behavior and the other's response to it. It's never just one thing.

And youngsters like me didn't have the foggiest notion what all the cat-human interaction is supposed to entail. Initially when they expressed interest in me, I had hoped it would be like my relationship with Fran. Ah, if only I could have been able to act upon the foreboding I had felt resulting from Jack, Betty, and Judy's interaction at the adoption clinic. If only I could have prevented this adoption from hell.

Time passed slowly. I walked around the house in the foot-deep snow to see if the back door were open for me. It wasn't. I waited ... and waited. I thought about curling up on the carpet under their new chair, enjoying the warmth of the blazing fire in the fireplace. I had been here so little time. Having had to repeatedly travel to and from adoption clinic and being gawked at in a cage now seemed like a mere trifle by comparison. I missed Fran who had been good to me as more than my foster mom. I was again getting hungry. Languishing in the cold, damp, dark dumpster came back in a flash. Maybe when things would become calmer inside and they would call me in for dinner and we could calmly retire to our respective corners. I'd cheerfully let them take me back to the clinic Maybe it would be soon.

More time passed. When they didn't call me in for dinner, I began to worry. As the sun slipped below the horizon, the temperature fell. I thought more about dying in the dumpster and worried even more about not being invited back in. It seemed that something must be terribly wrong. Could they have forgotten about me already?

I scratched at the large wooden front door with my icy-wet paws. I loudly meowed my apology for my accidents and everything else they thought I had done. I knew they were furious with me. I had no idea how *not* to provoke them. I knew they could, and likely would, hurt me again when I did something they didn't like. I also knew I didn't want to stay outside any longer. My short-haired coat wasn't going to keep me warm. Besides, there wasn't much of a fat layer beneath it for further insulation. Conflict and fear fought for my attention.

I continued to scratch, slap the door with my paws, and meow. But the door stayed closed. I made my way around the house seeking windows I could peer in. Perched on the sill of a living room window, I tried to peek in. The Venetian blinds were drawn. I pawed at the double-hung window panes anyway, making screeching noises with my claws to attract their attention. There was no response inside.

Were they still home? Had they gone out? I hadn't heard them leave. Didn't they hear me? I was getting colder. It was time to find something to shelter me from the harsh winter winds which were starting to blow from the east. Luckily, there was a small corrugated cardboard box they had emptied lying on the front porch on its side. I tentatively entered it and curled up as I waited for the front door to finally open. It was getting frigid. I had neither a blanket to snuggle into nor any fire to warm me. The leaves that had collected on the porch, which could have acted to reduce the transfer of my body heat, had long since been blown away. What would my mama do in this situation? I thought of my mother. I thought of the dumpster and cried.

Without warmth and protection I was in danger of my body temperature dipping too low, as it nearly did in the dumpster. I would freeze to death. What should I do? I was stymied about my next step. I napped only intermittently because the cold kept waking me. If they didn't open the door soon, I would have to try to paw and meow repeatedly to get their attention.

I wanted to believe they simply didn't realize I was there ready to come in and do whatever was necessary to make things okay until they could return me. They could get their adoption fee back. They could donate my minimal cat paraphernalia to the rescue group, or to Goodwill and take it as a deduction on their taxes, as I'd heard people had done. They could have the carpet cleaned where I'd accidentally done my business. The scratch on the chair which was barely visible could be repaired. But the next morning the blinds went up but no one responded to me pawing. The door stayed shut.

Another day passed as I coiled in my cardboard box, limbs stiffening. I had never known such cold before, even in the dumpster. I began venturing out in the leg-deep frozen precipitate only to eat some snow and pick up remnants of bird seed. The seed had fallen from the clear, nearly empty, cylindrical plastic bird feeder which hung from a low mulberry tree branch near the walkway. The seed looked years' old and dry but I was so hungry. Constant shivering had set in. I was feeling weak and sad.

What should I do? I didn't want to leave the front porch because Jack and Betty might open the door to take me in again. However, at the same time, if they didn't, I had to begin looking for food, water, and a warmer place to sleep in order to survive. I needed my mama; I needed Fran. I was just too young to know what to do next. My paws were sore from continually slapping the bottom of the wooden door and from being cold and wet. I licked them as dry as I could.

After another day, Jack and Betty reluctantly did check on me. If I still had been there on the porch, it was clear they were going to take me immediately back to the rescue group, give them a piece of their mind, threaten a possible law suit for the "damage" I caused, and get their refund. Going back would have been heaven. Maybe I'd go back with Fran ... even though I knew she had no room for me. However, when they opened the door, I was already across their large, snow-covered yard.

My mind started clicking in nanoseconds. Should I turn around and go back? I had left to try to save myself. What if they closed the door before I could leap through the snow to get to it? Would they open it again if I yowled to announce myself? Or would they just say "Good riddance to bad rubbish" and ignore me? I had already begun my journey as an outside cat. I was taking my survival into my own paws. Could I rely upon these humans to do the right thing?

Sixty seconds had barely passed as I had turned myself around and started back, bouncing through the snow to the house. As I approached the rear of the house, I heard Jack's angry shouting, "So you left? You goddamn, ungrateful cat! Boy that was money wasted. If that's the way you want it, you'd better keep the hell out of my sight ... or else!" The door slammed with a shock wave of finality.

That was definitive. I had no recourse now. Unfortunately, I hadn't an inkling where the adoption clinic or Fran's apartment was or I'd have tried to reach one or the other or both. As a kitten, I hadn't yet developed the purported skill of following electromagnetic fields, or whatever it was, that some cats who apparently found their way home used to guide them. Or was that mythology?

I knew I'd never see Fran or the adoption clinic again. I was totally on my own, being forced to learn how to beg and scrounge for food and find shelter wherever I went. I was being forced to learn how to deal with being chased by humans and other animals. I was being forced to quickly become an adult cat.

But as sorry as I was feeling for myself, I didn't want to emulate Blanche Dubois in Fran's favorite play "A Streetcar Named Desire." It was dangerous to operate on the magical concept that this is an ideal, sensitive world that will take care of you: "I have always depended on the kindness of strangers." I had already learned that reality was stark and often brutal.

In spite of that, it was still my deepest hope that someday I would encounter humans who would show compassion for a cat in my circumstance. In my imaginings they were not only helpful but also empathetic and welcoming. As I took on the struggle to make a new life for myself, it was increasingly obvious that the odds of finding what I wanted were against me.

Over the next weeks and months desperation motivated me to learn survival skills fast. Most of the time, I could dodge rocks thrown at me by children and teens. Invariably I saw or heard them first and read their intentions from their body language. When they tried to catch me, I was faster, more athletic, and smaller than they were. This permitted me to jump higher and duck quickly under and around refuse cans and cars. Staying alert was priority number one. I needed to be on my guard at all times.

Using pack predation methods, large dogs which were running wild around the adjacent neighborhoods chased and attacked me. Cats who wanted me out of their territory went after me as well. When I was caught unawares, brooms struck me across my back. Men kicked and cursed me for me digging in their yards and defecating in their gardens. Arrows aimed at my head or heart barely whipped past me. I was nearly roadkill time and again as cars, motorcycles, and bicycles did their best *not* to avoid me. From my life education to date I knew to be particularly afraid of what humans might do if they had me in their sights or, heaven forbid, caught me. This time it wouldn't likely have been merely dropping me into a dumpster to leave me to expire from hypothermia.

In a matter of a few months my fur had become rough-looking from my inadequate personal grooming. The area above my tail was greasy-looking with clumped, matted hair. On my tail were gaping, angry-looking areas where young boys had thrown lighted firecrackers at me, burning my fur and skin. Moreover, my face and body had become covered with the white lines and white patches of scars from all sorts of animal blitz attacks. I was frequently forced to do battle to protect myself and my territory which contained my few food resources. I didn't like fighting but when necessity called, I had to answer.

After having been booted out of my newly-adopted home into the snow, I was feeling more than slightly depressed. Don't let anyone tell you homeless cats can't or don't get depressed. They can and they do. But they don't have the luxury of whining about it or wallowing in self-pity. When you're a homeless cat, or, I suspect, a homeless human, you can't give in to depression when your life depends upon your keeping yourself sharp and your wits about you. You figure out exactly what basics you need and pursue them with all deliberation.

Finding food had been tough. I had to learn where I might be successful and then how to actually get it. I'd go after mice, birds, lizards, and snakes but often half-heartedly because I had no idea what I was doing. Besides, they didn't seem like food. My mom hadn't had the chance to teach me to dispatch mice so I really sucked at hunting. Exactly how was I supposed to plant a death bite on anything that moved or deal with a mouthful of fur, scales, or feathers from creatures that broke away from me? Even when a bird unknowingly flew down in front of me, I rarely went after it. Sure, its movement interested me but I didn't associate it with salving my hunger. I still warmly recalled and could almost taste the canned food Fran gave me with its gravy and hidden vegetables.

In desperation, especially when small creatures were harder to find in the cold and I was still learning what to do with them, I resorted on numerous occasions to chewing on rocks. Not only did they not address my hunger pangs, because I obviously couldn't swallow them, but also they broke off several teeth in the process. I was fortunate not to have constant mouth pain as a result.

Despite everything, I had somehow survived being homeless—although, just barely—whereas many other cats and dogs didn't. And then there were those poor dogs that were chained outdoors, abandoned, left to face weather extremes, neither homeless nor with a home. It was better to be a cat on my own. At least I was free. I stood a chance and would die trying.

One day when a full-grown German Shepherd chased me as I ran across an icy street, I knew I was in trouble. He had spotted me first, from behind a mailbox, giving him a head start. Before I could say, "Pretty Polly picked a peck of purple peppers," this cur had locked its jaws on my head, my face in his mouth. Wet saliva dripped in my eyes and nose. The vice-like pressure of his jaws was crumbling the cartilage in my right ear which would later cause it to flop over as if I were wearing a hat at a jaunty angle. Slashing at his eyes with my front claws and raking his throat with my hind feet, I managed to motivate him to let me go. He had a choice to make: hang onto my head or scream in exquisite pain. As a consequence, when I escaped, I looked even more battle-scarred, shabby, and much older than I really was.

Over the next several months I had drifted some five miles from my first "almost-home." Despite all I had endured since kitten-hood, I was still a friendly cat—wary of humans at first then gradually accepting of their touch. I had come to trust only a few humans, allowing them to get really close to me. For others who left me open cans of cat food or tuna, bowls of cat chow, human food from the dinner table, water, and a blanket-padded, sheltered place to sleep, I thanked them from a short distance.

I often wondered why they didn't extend their help to offering me a home. They couldn't *all* be "allergic" to cats. Come on, even though I know that some people are feline allergic, that's usually just a pathetic excuse for not wanting to take the responsibility of providing a cat with a home. In spite of it all, when someone offered food, I made sure to sit on their front walk lifting my whiskers and tail to send them a loud "thank you" meow. Reciprocity and gratitude are cat watch words.

One person whom I trusted to both feed and pet me was a nine-year-old, hearing-impaired girl named Thursa. She lived in a yellow house with dark green shutters, door, and trim at the middle of a treed cul-de-sac off Rockland. I visited her every morning before she went to school. I meowed my greeting and pawed the back screen door. As soon as Thursa's mother heard me, she alerted Thursa, "Tom's here." Any name was as good as another. Thursa then brought a dish of dry cat chow and a bowl of water out to me. This was our routine. She cheerily greeted me then sat on the back stairs, petting and talking to me while I appreciatively ate and drank. She never invited me inside.

Every weekday I followed Thursa to school. She was in fourth grade. I could see she hated interacting with the unimpaired-hearing kids her age. Sitting on the playground periphery, I had seen that at first they were curious about the obvious hearing aids she wore. Then her classmates began to make fun of the clunky-looking instruments. They sometimes laughed at the nasality of her voice and their occasional difficulty discerning her words. They mimicked her. Curiosity had quickly been replaced by bullying: ongoing insulting comments and derisive laughter.

As I watched each Monday through Friday before going on my food rounds, I couldn't understand this behavior. Why were they picking on her? Irrespective of reasons they may have given, it was cruel. She was already a victim ... but even if she hadn't been ... She apparently didn't understand either. She just wanted to be accepted, to have friends. As a result, she came to loathe wearing the hearing aids, indicating with hot tears running down her red, squeezed face, she wanted to stomp on them and crush them to tiny bits underfoot.

This Saturday morning she was firm, she told me as I watched her body language and listened to her tone. She had decided she was going to go without her hearing aids. By doing so, she was going to prove to everyone, but especially to herself, that she didn't really need them. Without them, she would no longer give her classmates anything to laugh at. She could make them stop. They could become her friends at last. They would play and have fun together. She wouldn't be lonely any longer.

When her mother arrived from grocery shopping and pulled the car into the garage, Thursa was still wearing her hearing aids. She helped bring in the ten paper bags of foodstuffs from the garage. But as soon as her mother was pre-occupied with putting the groceries away, Thursa slipped off her hearing aids. She left them on the passenger seat and walked quickly out of the garage into the side yard. As she sat on the still-dew-covered grass, I stood in front of her. Behind her the cascading golden boughs of forsythia swayed in the slight breeze which likewise carried the lilting fragrance of the white puffballs of viburnum on either side of the front door in our direction.

I usually hung around Thursa's house on weekends after breakfast to keep her company. Being with her was refreshing. Unlike so many adults, she seemed to listen and be able to understand me even if she couldn't actually hear me. Her distress about her hearing aids was palpable. More and more she had become socially isolated. Through her bedroom window I could see she spent a great deal of time alone reading books by Judy Blume or playing old video games, like *Myst*. She wasn't on social media any longer because the negative comments and bullying continued there. She hardly went out except with her parents to the zoo, sports events, or shopping. She used to go to the movies which she loved, identifying with the characters and escaping. As a result, Saturday evenings were special.

But as the bullying escalated, she went less frequently with her parents because her classmates were likely to be there as well. They would stare, talk among themselves, point, and snicker. It didn't matter how much she wanted to see the movie. It was too embarrassing.

She no longer attended any school dances. She felt she was looked upon as a freak. No one would dance with her. Occasionally a boy who approached her was quickly pulled aside by friends who clued him into the resulting negative social effect of doing so. Sitting alone at the side of the gym, while everyone else danced, made her the focus of everyone's attention. She worried her bullies might even treat her like Stephen King's "Carrie," with a bucket of pig's blood.

While her parents had initially tried to force then encourage her to go, she became too distressed and despondent. They so wanted her to enjoy her childhood and, especially, have friends but that wasn't happening. They worried endlessly how that would affect her emotionally later on. They had suggested a school for the hearing impaired which she vehemently refused. She didn't want to go to school with people who were disabled and see herself assigned that label too.

On weekends when she was not doing homework, reading, or doing chores, she spent most of her afternoons looking out the living room window. In general as I sauntered away to resume my daily feeding schedule after several hours with her, I could see her watching the birds flitting from maple to maple or pulling out worms from the new-growth grass in the side yard. She watched the squirrels scampering on the lawn, fighting with companions over acorns they had dug up from last year's hiding places. I interpreted it as her longing to freely explore the world on her own like her furry and feathered friends. She must know, or at least suspect, there was so much out there she could discover. And maybe she could do it some day without emotional pain.

As I sat with Thursa on the grass, she seemed distressed and talked to me at length. "Wha is yo liv lik? Is id an aventu? Ah yu habby?" I had never paid attention to the frequent indistinctness of her words. I didn't need to. Her tone, inflection, and body language told me much of what I needed to know about her thoughts, attitudes, and feelings. Other messages from her seemed to simply materialize in my head. In response I generally cocked my head and meowed, even though without her hearing aids this morning she couldn't pick up the sounds.

However, this morning, I continued to rub against her legs, my body vibrating to show my understanding and affection for her. She always grinned broadly at my touch, as if finding it comforting. She lavishly petted me and I resonated to her touch as well. I'd never given her being mostly inarticulate much thought. It was just the way she was. That's how I looked at things, as I suspect most cats looked at things. It was what she communicated to me in other ways that truly mattered.

When Thursa finished her petting session with me, she took on a look of determination. Standing up, the seat of her jeans damp from the dew, she threw her shoulders back and marched out of her yard onto the sidewalk toward town. Her posture suggested she was obviously feeling emboldened, having discarded her awkward hearing amplification apparatus. She was about to embark on an exciting, new adventure. She was being independent and doing it all on her own terms ... like me ... for the first time. Filled with concern, I decided to follow, walking behind her.

As she passed the third house on the left, a white Victorian with dark blue trim, a large dog, a Rhodesian Ridgeback named Herman, raced toward her, barking. His collar was attached to a chain which was on a long wire strung twenty-five feet or so between two tall trees. She didn't notice the dog until he had stopped at the end of his tether, raised up on his hind legs at the concrete's edge.

Surprised by what had seemed like an attack, she fell backward onto the sidewalk, crab-walk scrambling to get out of the dog's reach. Herman, however, wasn't trying to attack her. He was tied up outside all day all by himself. He was lonesome too. Whenever he saw someone who could pay him some attention, perhaps play with him, he raced up to them.

But shocked by the suddenness of the incident, Thursa seemed unsure what the dog's behavior signaled. As she tried to right herself, her knees buckle under her. Regaining an upright position, she turned and ran down the sidewalk toward the cross street, her navy blue Keds making a rapid slapping sound. Herman looked after her with forlorn eyes. Slowly he walked back to the back yard where he lay down again under the old oak, looking defeated, his head draped on his front paws.

Thursa raced across the street without looking. Fortunately no cars were in view. Her destination was downtown. She had never been this far all on her own before. The school that she walked to was less than a block away from her home in the other direction. It required no street crossing.

After several more blocks, she was surrounded by the hustle and bustle of vehicles and human traffic, everyone in action with purpose and specific destinations in mind. Everything seemed to be moving fast all around her yet all was silent. She paused, raised her chin, and straightened her back. She began to casually glance around, first at the traffic then at the stores as if it were part of her *normal* everyday life. She felt so adult and so free. It was a wonderful feeling. She relished it.

I trotted closely behind her with a sense of apprehension. Where was she going? What was she going to do? As long as I had known her, which was almost a year's time, she had never done anything like this before. But then again she had never been nine years old before … or bullied so badly before. While I had my regular schedule to follow, today I decided to skip it.

Through my constant territorial travel, I had established myself as a fixture: well-known and, apparently, well-liked in the neighborhood among homeowners and business owners alike. It was comforting to know that there were kind humans who expected me and were always on the lookout for me. Some put out dishes of food for me as I passed by. Others would smile, say something pleasant, and maybe give me along sensuous pat on the back. I'd lift my whiskers and wave my raised tail in response. We connected in one way or another. That was gratifying.

Thursa had begun to look in store windows at all the wares that were being offered. The window displays seemed to fascinate her. There were books, dresses, cakes, bicycles, electric drills, and dog beds. Stores here looked so different from the stores in the mall, less slick, more individual. As she walked slowly along, marveling at the variety of what was for sale, a young boy who was wobbly riding a girl's bicycle that was too big for him was approaching quickly behind her. He was ringing his bell at her, warning her to get out of the way. It was obvious he was not sure he could maneuver around her successfully. But she didn't hear its clanging.

I screeched a blood-curdling yowl at the top of my lungs from his right. It had the desired effect. He changed direction slightly to the left, away from me. Of course, Thursa didn't hear me. Instead of hitting her straight on, the boy only bumped her elbow with the right rubber handle grip as he swept past her. She jumped forward, slightly doubled over, landing against the plate glass store front and hitting her head.

I walked up to her, wrapped my tail around her legs to comfort her. She was quite shaken. "Oooo," she moaned as she massaged her skull. She took a few moments to get her breath then turned to face the sidewalk. Surprised to find me there, she knelt down to embrace me as an old reliable friend. I tried nudging her with my body so that she should follow me. She stood but didn't move. Maybe she didn't understand. I tried again. No result. This time I sat on my haunches and grabbed at her pant legs. Slapping, I caught the fabric and tried to pull her along as I moved forward along the sidewalk. There seemed to be something wrong although I didn't know what it was. Why wasn't she responding to me? I looked at her with a semblance of kitty concern covering my scarred face.

Thursa looked down at me and I could see her thoughts play out on her face. Pain and confusion were passing. Replacing them were the pros and cons of following me. By comparison with her life, my life was one big adventure. I was free to go my own way, do whatever I wanted, and do it whenever I wanted. After all, I wasn't tied down to school. I didn't have to wear humiliating hearing aids. I didn't have children laughing at me all the time. She was right to a degree but she was too young to see the other side of my so-called "devil-may-care, adventurous" life.

As I continued to pull at her left pant leg, she made up her mind. Rather than continue on her own, she was going to follow me, keeping one step behind, like my shadow. That meant that I had to pay particular attention to any neighborhood or stray dogs and cats. Whenever any animal came near or its body language indicated it might do so, I arched my back, stiffened my hair, and raised my bushed out tail. I signaled them I was moving precious cargo and would brook no interference. Step out of line and I was going to be their worst nightmare. This was a side of me that Thursa had not seen before. I could see her respect for me grow.

When we came to a large intersection at the end of the block, Thursa saw the red light for cars, and started to step off the curb. But she had missed seeing the traffic on her left, on the street perpendicular to the street she was facing. It had been given the green light to turn right. It was coming toward her. As she was about to step off the curb, I slipped in front of her diagonally to nudge her and stop her from crossing. She stumbled back. Immediately I began pawing at her leg, distracting her, until the turning traffic had passed. Then I proceeded, once again, guiding her with my body and paws.

In the next thirty minutes I had managed to reverse our direction and lead her back to her yard. Mr. Spock would have been proud of what our mind meld had accomplished. There her distraught mother was in their driveway talking to police she had called about her "missing" daughter. When we arrived, she greeted Thursa with great bear hug and a look of tearful relief.

When I saw these strangers in black uniforms, wearing guns, Tasers, handcuffs, and clubs, I immediately took my position in front of Thursa. If she needed protection from them, I was it. Bring it on! But they didn't move toward us. When her mother released her, I assisted Thursa with my tail and body toward her open garage door so she could collect her hearing aids.

Thursa's mother followed me with her eye, shaking her head questioningly. I could tell she was asking herself if I had *followed* Thursa back or if I had actually *brought* her back. Chuckling, she knew she'd never know for sure what the truth was. Suddenly I spotted something that portended a new life. Thursa's mother had had an aha! A smile graced her face. There was an obvious recognition that Thursa and I had a very special bond—a communication beyond hearing. It was something she badly wanted to cultivate for her lonely child.

What this meant was that just maybe I could—more to the point, should—become Thursa's "hearing-ear cat." When she was with me, she didn't seem to worry about her hearing aids. Yes, I was her loved and trusted companion, even her BFF. That meant I should come live with her, starting right now. I looked into Thursa's eyes, lifted my whiskers and shouted silently over my shoulder to her mother, Good move. Works for me.

§ § §

CHAPTER 5

CHARLEY

I'm Charley, a female, long-haired, autumn-shaded Tortoiseshell—Torties are almost exclusively female. An elder by most kitty standards, I'm seventeen years old. That's the equivalent of eighty-four in human years. I keep myself fit, don't eat quiche, whipped cream, or caviar leftovers. Well, that is, I wouldn't even if I came upon them in the garbage bin behind the small town's only four-star restaurant. I hadn't always been on my own. For over sixteen years I had been friend-therapist-companion to a wonderful female human, Caryn, who doted on me. No kidding. But what was even better was that we could read each other's minds. It was a dream-come-true relationship.

Then she became ill at the end of spring. She no longer could make decisions for herself ... or for me. She had no family but me, and I couldn't read and sign contracts. I had no standing in court to help her. That was very distressing and struck me as being discriminatory. So when she died, her lawyer was in charge of disposing of her "belongings," which inconceivably but legally included me. What an antediluvian and tacky concept. Most laws don't seem to cover the realities of human-companion animal relationships. We're not like a piece of property or real estate you can sell or put in storage when the "owner" dies.

The lawyer and I had never really gotten along. The legal eagle was one of those humans who carry lint rollers with them. Acting as his own valet service, he constantly used them to disinfect his apparel even though I had no white hair to decorate his dark suits. Whether or not he actually ever had any physical contact with me, he was always whipping out his plastic bottle of hand sanitizer to clean his hands when I was near. What a chuckle! I was undoubtedly cleaner than anything else he would touch. I'll bet he didn't wash his hands after using the bathroom. What a gigantic dog turd. Just to make the point that he was unwelcome, whenever he came into the house, I would start doing figure eights around his ankles as he tried to walk. Stumbling over me, I'm sure he thought it was a sign of affection. For someone else it might well have been. But I was taking control, demonstrating whose domicile this really was, and interfering with his entry into it. Get the message, dummy?

When Caryn died, he had shown no interest whatsoever in finding me another place to live. At least the person he had hired to clean and straighten up the place had fed me and cleaned my litter. I had heard him inquire on the phone about the cost of "putting Charley down." When he asked it, he stared at me and curled his upper lip in disgust, as if smelling boiling cabbage. No question about his threatening, aggressive intent. It was *Hasta la vista*, Charley, baby. I didn't have to know what precisely he meant to do with me, but it was likely not to be good for a feisty, gorgeous Tortie, "in the pink" with my golden years still ahead of me.

I wanted to hang around a while longer and smell the catmint. It occurred to me that I'd better relocate where he would have difficulty finding and getting hold of me to follow through on his proposed evil deed. I waited for the right moment. During one of his many visits after that phone call, I slipped out of the house and disappeared. In fact, that was easy to do since the lawyer didn't give a crap about me, and rarely paid more than cursory attention to me. Stick that in your hat, Bozo. Not that I thought he'd really care. Gone is gone. Now he had something less he had to deal with.

Since I was primarily an indoor cat except when Caryn took me for walks in a harness and leash, I knew a lot of her neighbors around us. But following the same routes I'd taken with Caryn, now without her and the leash and harness for safety and security, I was a lot more timid and vulnerable. No cat wants to feel vulnerable. I didn't want to be seen as weak, sporting a sandwich board with "Victim here" printed in flashing neon lights.

Caryn had been gone nearly two weeks. I wandered around, at my wits' end, doing what I did half-heartedly, keeping an eye open for the lawyer, just in case. But I felt as if a cannonball had blown a hole in my gut large enough for a Hummer to drive through. My heart had been crushed in the process. Of all the things I had to think about as a result of her demise having a place to live was not a top priority. It was early summer. But still I needed what "home" meant to me. I craved that. Most of all, I wanted my treasured human companion, Caryn, back.

One morning as I was sauntering by eighty-three-year-old Abner Witherspoon's house, two houses down from Caryn's, I heard the disconcerting high-pitched chorus of scratchy miniature wails. Young kittens were calling for their mother. Following the sound, I found it was emanating from under Abner's long white wooden front porch. There I discovered five little balls of feline fluff that apparently had been weaned and were plaintively demanding some grub ... now. But where was their mother? Was she out hunting? No, that didn't make sense.

Abner *always* left dishes of canned food out on the porch for cats—any cats. They could be feral, neighborhood cats, or "once-upon-a-time neighborhood cats." So many felines had been cavalierly dumped, left to fend for themselves, when the economy was bad, or their humans had tired of them or just moved away. Somehow those individuals managed to convince themselves that their cats could take care of themselves. Yeah, right. It was like dropping a child off at the side of the road and told, "Do whatever you can to survive."

Something was wrong with this picture. I left them for a moment to explore Abner's yard just in case she had left for some other reason. When I arrived in the back yard, Oh, damn! There I found the kittens' tabby mother. She was dead but unbloodied. She probably had been killed by some stupid dog holding her by her neck, shaking and tossing her around like a ragdoll as a form of play until she expired. I sniffed her body and touched her shoulder with my paw. Mama cat was still warm and supple so she had been dead much less than an hour. Damn, damn, damn! That made the situation difficult.

Abner lived in his large house all alone since his wife, Lydia, had died the year before. Except for greeting neighbors along the street, especially Caryn and me, or working on his flower beds, he had become a semi-recluse. I knew there was still some canned food currently available on the porch since I'd had a snack earlier. But how, I wondered, was I going to get these rambunctious little ones to it. I let out a loud howl to see if Abner were home so I could direct him to his visitors. But I heard no response.

If you think herding cats is tough, you ought to try herding kittens. I tried to entice the little dust bunnies to follow me out from under the porch and up the stairs onto it. It was an exercise in futility. It was even worse than trying to get most humans to follow your directions, no matter how simple and clear-cut they were. It never ceases to amaze me how some humans simply cannot walk and chew at the same time. I'm surprised they have survived as long as they have as a species.

Up and down the stairs I trod, trying to get the noisy packets of energy to follow me. Finally I employed their mother's maneuver of grabbing them by the scruff of their necks and carrying them as their mother would. Believe me, this is not an instinctive behavior for an old single female cat. It was measure of last resort.

Capturing them was a multi-step process because they were constantly heading off in one direction or another. The "mommy maneuver" seemed easy enough in theory … until I clamped on. They were heavier than they looked. And their bodies hung low, swaying back and forth, scraping the ground, and thumping as I awkwardly lugged them step-by-step up the four stairs to the food.

There I urged the congregated roiling mass to eat—yum, yum, yum—the soft, moist meaty food. Some needed more encouragement than others. Those who stumbled onto the food were doing a two-step in the Friskies, knocking over the paper plates, mock fighting. One plowed ahead, falling face-first into the Poultry Platter. I was glad I wasn't a mother. It took all my patience and resolve to keep pushing these mindless creatures back to the once-again-righted plates. Their mother would have made sure they ate, each one getting its fair share. Each had to thrive. Responsibility is a heavy burden but I vowed no kitten was going to fade and die on my watch.

When they had more or less finished their meal, I did what I was expected to do. I cleaned each of them of food remnants with my rough, pink tongue. Several of the kittens thought this was game time and grabbed hold of my face with their talons and hung on. Others crawled on my body to explore or curl up on me. Gently I detached the horde, pawed at them to gather them around my warm belly to have their afternoon nap. After they checked out my nipples and found nothing to suckle, they dropped off. Before the sun went down, I would have to lead them back under the porch for their protection.

After Caryn died and before discovering the kittens, I had stopped by Abner's regularly once a day. Sometimes Abner saw me and came out to talk. Now with a family in tow I had to stop by Abner's several times a day. The kittens needed to eat, play, and begin their cat education.

Their first lesson needed to take place on the grass. Here I showed them how to lie quietly in wait for a grasshopper before pouncing on it. They already could pounce just fine. Boy oh boy, couldn't they just. Waiting quietly, however, before doing it totally eluded them. They wanted to inspect each grass blade and wrestle with their brothers and sisters, leaping into the air with paws spread-eagle. What a distracted and distractible bunch. After a wearying hour, they sort of got the gist or, more likely, were just too exhausted to continue to play.

Once they had somewhat achieved that skill, I moved onto mice. I don't know how mothers do it. Maybe it comes with hormones, like so-called "nest-building"/bonding oxytocin, and hard-wired instinct. You couldn't prove it by me. Anyway, here I demonstrated that they had to catch the mouse by the neck so they could kill it quickly. I found that this skill likewise far exceeded their abilities at this stage of their development. After having been an indoor cat since kitten-hood, I wasn't exactly that proficient at it either. But irrespective—

How they executed the new techniques, or tried to, was, however, endearing. I had corralled one poor mouse for "show-and-tell." Let loose and facing the anticipating horde, it stood stock still, its black eyes bulging even more, its whiskers twitching. On my "Go!" signal the kittens mock-charged—if you could call it that. Their lack of focus and incoordination was almost comical. As all five casually approached, still checking out insects at their feet, the mouse became disoriented. Instead of scampering away, it ran straight toward them. The kittens screeched and fell all over themselves and their siblings, trying to escape the attacking pursuit of this huge rodent beast.

After a week of teaching the kittens the basics of cat-hood as I knew them, I had them follow me onto the porch in order to meet Abner. They needed to learn to socialize with humans. One important proviso in dealing with humans was that humans didn't necessarily do what cats do. Specifically, even though as cats they sniffed each other's butts for recognition, they should not expect a human to reciprocate. While this might seem insulting, it was just a human eccentricity that they had to accept.

Demonstrating how acrobatics training could also come in handy later on, I gracefully leapt up to the door handle and swung to and fro. As my body slammed into the door, Abner shuffled his way to see what the commotion was about. Before him on the door sill was a surprise. It was me and my adopted tabby-patterned brood.

"Well, well. What have we here? Are these yours, Charley?" The kittens looked up at him in anticipation. "No, I would have seen you pregnant. Besides, they don't look like you. I am so sorry about Caryn." He began rambling again, something that was more evident every day. "You must feel about losing her as I do about losing my Lydia. Lydia and I too loved cats. When our last cat, twenty-two-year-old Moffet, died, I swore I'd never have another cat. It's just too painful. I think Lydia actually died of a broken heart after Moffet." Abner stopped as his eyes began to fill.

"But enough of that. How about you all come in? I can give you something special. Maybe a little tuna fish. What do you say, Charley?" His voice was encouraging and foretold of something tasty.

As Abner retreated into his kitchen to open several cans of chunk-style tuna which he put on Desert Rose-patterned lunch plates, I led the kittens into his front hall. It was obvious that my protégés were not responding to my direction but to the enticing aroma wafting their way. I had never been invited inside before by myself. It was always with Caryn. But then again there had never been any reason for me to have done so, until now.

The kittens slurped up the tuna broth while I had only a small mouthful of the meat. Instead of continuing to eat, I kept nudging the kittens toward the two dishes Abner had put on the floor. I was so grateful that Abner had taken such an interest in the little ones that I rubbed my face and body against his leg. I was hoping he would feel the pull of the gravity of these little ones being on their own and find a way to take them under his wing.

Abner was engrossed in all that the kittens did, a smile creasing his cheeks. Then he looked at me and asked, "What are you saying to me, huh, Charley? Why did you bring your little adopted family to see me?" I continued to rub against Abner to hear me tell him that the kittens needed him. "Are you asking me to take care of these babies? You know I can't do that. I'm too old. You know my beloved Moffet died... then Lydia. I can't go through that again. You can rub against me all you want, but I can't—I won't—do it." His voice cracked.

There was a long pause as Abner disappeared into another world. A gauze curtain seemingly dropped over his face. When he returned, he looked around for the kittens. By now they had filled their little bellies and had scattered all around the living room and hall. The brown tabby was climbing into Abner's potted philodendron sitting on a side table. Its heart-shaped leaves cascaded over the edge to the red and black area rug below. He'd have to be removed because the leaves were poisonous if chewed. The tan tabby had scooted under his faded floral sofa. It was popping its head out in eagerness as if playing peek-a-boo. The orange tabby and its black-stripped sibling were unsuccessfully attempting to climb the red-carpeted stair treads to the second floor. And the last one, the gray and white runt of the litter, was attempting to scale Abner's chino pant leg.

It wouldn't be long before it was kitten chaos. Small furry bodies would be getting into everything. He would be finding little fur balls in the garbage and laundry basket, under the bed, in the closets. They would be constantly underfoot. They would knock everything onto the floor. They would unroll toilet paper and tear it into tiny pieces. They would perch on his newspaper as he tried to read the local news and Dear Abby. They would try to enter his refrigerator and re-arrange socks in his sock drawer. If he were lucky, they wouldn't learn how to flush the toilet or turn on the kitchen faucet for a drink.

Abner detached the small fur ball from his leg and held it in his hand, closely examining it. The kitten reached out for Abner's nose, grabbed it with both paws, and began snuggling with it. Abner smiled again, tentatively at first. Then his face broke into a beatific grin. This was something I had not seen since before Moffet had left them.

I sat by quietly while Abner focused on the feline barbarians that had invaded his lonely castle. He steepled his hands then rested them on his lips as if in deep thought. Then pretending to be frustrated with their behaviors, he began to follow them around the living room and hall. As he moved, his shuffle seemed to disappear. He was walking with the smallest spring to his step. One by one he lovingly scooped them into his arms then deposited them on his sofa cushions where he sat next to them. Tenderly he played with them to keep them from jumping or falling off onto the floor.

Still seated in the hall, I looked at him. Abner saw me and theatrically exclaimed, "Okay, Charley, I give up. You have me beaten. I'll take them in. You win. But don't bring any more orphans to my door. There's only me to take care of them now. Do we have a deal?" He smiled as if he had a secret. I lifted my whiskers in recognition of the incandescent glow spreading over Abner's face.

Pulling a shoelace from his Rockports to keep the kittens occupied, Abner rose and walked to the door. "And don't worry about them. You can visit them any time you like. And ...don't you worry about my continuing to feed you. I'll keep putting out your plate of food." My heart sank. I had hoped the invitation to stay included me. It didn't. Despite my disappointment, I walked with my head and tail held high to the still-ajar door and left.

The next day I continued my scheduled rounds. Daylight was fading as I circled back toward my old home, where I had taken to bivouacking under the floriferous white dogwood tree Caryn and I planted so many years ago. I thought I might stop by Abner's to see what his adopted family was doing. Were they outside playing? I hoped not. They needed the safety and protection of indoors. They needed monitoring. I was sure Abner knew that but just to be sure I checked under the porch then surveyed his back yard.

Fresh soil told me Abner had buried the kittens' mother next to Moffett. Moffett had been placed at the foot of the blooming, fragrant yellow azaleas which graced his shady six-foot back fence. Since the kittens appeared to be inside, I went to the front door to make my presence known. As I pawed at the door, I smelled something unpleasant. What was that? It frightened me enough to make me want to cut and run.

I could hear the kittens inside mewing. Fortunately, Abner hadn't closed the front door tightly again so it was open an inch or so. That was very odd. I slipped inside. Oh, no! What I had smelled was smoke. It was coming from the kitchen. Running down the hall, I leapt onto the counter. From there I could see a burner was on under a metal pot. The pot had likely held some liquid in it that now was dry, burned, glowing, and red hot. A plastic stirring spoon, too close to the flame, was melting and heating a note pad on the counter. I had no idea what to do about it. I didn't know how to turn off the stove. I had no idea how to move the pot, spoon, or pad without burning myself or setting the curtains, counter, or floor on fire.

Instead I hopped down. Letting out a loud yowl, I went in search of the five youngsters. They were hiding everywhere. They looked confused and distraught. Speaking with them firmly but kindly, I took control and convinced them to follow me outside, through the front door gap. The automatic porch light was flickering on above them.

Then it struck me. Where was Abner? He had to be there. He wouldn't have put a pot on the stove to heat and left the house. And what humans said cats don't think? Having settled the kittens on the other end of the porch away from the door, I re-entered to begin to survey the house. Where to look? I went room by room on the lower level, shouting my presence as I went. There was no sign of Abner. I heard no signs of any human activity. The increasing smoke made the hair on my back bristle. My body was screaming at me to run away, escape the danger … immediately if not sooner. But I felt compelled, against my survival instinct, to find Abner first.

Cautiously I ascended the red-carpeted stairs. Abner had to be around. I meowed as loudly as I could. I kept telling myself he would never have left them voluntarily. Maybe he had fallen. Maybe he was ill. Maybe he was sleeping. Being a pragmatic cat, I didn't even consider the possibility of his having been kidnapped and held for ransom. How likely was that, I mean really. I checked out the two rooms on the left, screaming to alert Abner there was a problem. I found nothing. Still listening for any untoward sound, I retraced my steps to check out the rooms on the right, doing my championship best high-decibel yowl. I thought I had better find him soon because I was losing my voice from the heavy particulate matter that was drifting up the stairs.

It was there in the second room that I saw Abner stretched out on the bed. I jumped onto the bedspread and crawled onto his stomach. I began kneading his stomach, meowing. Abner didn't respond. I crawled onto his chest and kneaded some more, harder, screeching loud enough to wake the neighborhood. There was still no response. At this point I sat in front of Abner's face and pawed it. I slapped his cheeks as if I were telling another cat in no uncertain terms that this was *my* territory so buzz off. Abner began to stir. I kept it up, meowing and slapping harder, mostly with my right paw. He moved and slowly awakened.

Clutching his chest, he moaned, "My heart. I think I may have had a heart attack. Oh, it's you, Charley? What are you doing here?"

It was then that the smell of smoke was getting stronger as it wound its way down the hall to his bedroom.

"Oh, my, what is that smell? Oh, no. I remember now. I put soup on for dinner. It must be the pot. Dear Lord, we have a fire! Let me see if I can get up."

Abner rose unsteadily. "I'd better go check out the kitchen to see what I can do to put out the fire. Then I'll call the fire department. Oh, my goodness! The kittens! I have to collect the kittens! We have to get them out of the house right away!" Abner was standing beside the bed. "Those poor little things. They must be scared sick. My God, a fire! I have to rescue them." He shuffled doing his version of a quick-step down the hall.

Abner tightly grabbed the railing as he made his way down the stairs with me in front of him. The hallway was now filled with smoke. Together we made our way through the charcoal-laced air to see that the paper had ignited, burned the aqua Formica countertop, spread to the yellow and white curtains. Tongues of fire were starting to slither up the flowered wallpaper and consume it, cackling and snapping as they did. The fire was still somewhat contained but growing fast. "I don't have a fire extinguisher any more. I used to have one and never replaced. Dumb, Abner, dumb!" I tried to get his attention to get another pot, fill it with water, and throw it at the wall. But he couldn't hear me.

Coughing and gasping, Abner made his way to the phone in the living room. He barely finished calling 911 as his voice began to fade. Then he snatched up a flashlight from the white wooden mantelpiece to look for the kittens. I tried to grab his pant leg to lead him to the front door where the kittens awaited him. But Abner didn't understand. He was too frightened and focused on his concern about the kittens to hear me. Dammit, Abner! Listen to *me*. But all Abner knew was that the kittens were in danger. They were his babies, his responsibility. He had to save them.

He wandered blindly from room to room, stumbling over furniture. He held a dry handkerchief to his mouth and nose and called the kittens to him. He waved the light around aimlessly. "Here, kitties! Come to Abner." His coughing and gasping were getting worse. He had to leave but he wouldn't leave the kittens behind. He couldn't bear for them to die. It was up to him and him alone to save them.

He staggered to the front door to call them to him. The fresh air could help direct the kittens to him and safety. But once at the door, he lost consciousness. Collapsing, his body doubled-over and slid to the red-and-black runner which was tacked on the wide-plank wooden floor. His shoulder landed against the front door, shutting it.

I tried pawing the edge of the door but couldn't get any purchase. I tried slapping Abner again, this time with claws exposed, hoping to revive him. But the carbon monoxide in the smoke had knocked him out. I even tried to shift his shoulder from the door to get it ajar again. A fool's errand, to be sure, but I was desperate. In spite of the greater amount of oxygen near the floor, it wasn't enough. I collapsed next to Abner. I lay like a lump, my breathing and heart rate slowing. Foam bubbled from my mouth.

Just then the fire department broke through the front door. Several rescuers pulled Abner to safety and gave him oxygen. It was only as the fire fighters sped to the kitchen with the fire hose that anyone saw my nearly lifeless body. One rescuer picked me up and raced me outside as well. There was only the slightest heartbeat, slow and unsteady. Fortunately the town had purchased animal-sized oxygen rescue masks to be available to every fire department, paramedics unit, and animal rescuers' group in the town. They were trained how to use them and give cardio-pulmonary resuscitation. Immediately they started me on oxygen as well. They knew that if they did not start oxygen right away, I was likely to die before they could reach the nearest emergency animal hospital.

A large, round-faced fire fighter named Jim strapped the mask over my face then began CPR. It took a few minutes before I was starting to breathe. Now my heart was beating faster. Jim kept up the oxygen therapy until I could open my eyes, stand, and walk on my own. At that point Jim shared with his colleague that most of the carbon monoxide was likely out of my system. My brain was fuzzy ... but I was alive!

Abner was lying on a gurney, now conscious. He had his own oxygen mask still in place but was talking through it, over the paramedics' objections. Things were moving fast. I jumped up and licked his face around the mask before the paramedics rolled him into an ambulance to take him to the hospital. Abner caught a glimpse of his five furry babies sitting quietly in a puddle of water on the other end of the front porch. "Charley, I don't know how you managed to get them out but you have my undying gratitude. Take care of them for me until I get home. Do whatever you have to do. Take them with you on your daily route. Caryn was very lucky to have had you. Thank you for being such a great cat."

I jumped down as Abner was being shut into the ambulance which pulled away from the curb and disappeared toward town with its lights flashing and siren whooping. Now it was again totally up to me to take care of the kittens. I looked at the wet porch and made my way to it. My "adopted" family was gathered together, waiting for me to decide what to do next. With them around me, I felt the burden weigh heavily. As I licked and groomed them despite some being dripping wet, the kittens nuzzled me. I sat there awhile marveling at all that had happened but glad Abner and the kittens had survived.

Then as if having made a plan, I gave them explicit instructions to follow me. Lining them up, I headed them down the porch steps and along the sidewalk to the right. We approached the first neighbors we saw, Mrs. Martin and her husband from next door. They had been watching the firefighters extinguish the blaze. Looking up at them, I looked as pathetic and begging as I could. Mrs. Martin had helped Abner with Lydia in her final days and later when Abner himself needed assistance after a couple of minor cardiac incidents. One or the other of them would greet Caryn and me on our walks. I was always guaranteed a good pet from them. When I locked my eyes with Mrs. Martin, I begged her, Please take care of us until Abner returns. It will only be a day or two. I wasn't sure if either had heard me.

They both were looking shocked at the bedraggled kittens. Mrs. Martin said, "Look at those poor babies. Were they Abner's?" Then she did a double-take. "Charley? Is that really you? What are you doing here? I thought for sure one of Caryn's distant relatives had taken you home with them after Caryn left us. I am *so* sorry about Caryn. Funny, I would never have guessed Abner had taken you in, given Lydia and Moffett. I wish—if only I'd known you had been available ..." Her sentence trailed off and she sighed. She and her husband looked at each other and smiled. "But we're so glad to see you. And that you're all well." Okay, I thought, then beam me up, Scottie. Yes, Caryn and I were big "Star Trek" fans.

Apparently they heard me because Mr. Marin started giving us directions, "Okay, you guys, let's all head to our house until Abner gets back home. You little ones are still wet and need to be dried. And, you, Charley, you smell of smoke. You need a bath." Shaking his head, he added, "It's absolutely amazing what you did for Abner and the kittens. Simply amazing. If Abner hadn't told us, we'd never have believed it. Who knew a cat could do all that. You remind us of our Toby ... the things he could do ... and how very much we miss him." Sniffing, he bent down toward the kittens.

I could have done without the bath part—although I did stink—but I was glad the kittens had a warm, dry place to sleep and food to eat until Abner returned. I lifted my whiskers to acknowledge acceptance of their kind offer. They both picked up the kittens and told me to follow. But as we walked to their house, I could feel my whiskers droop. I wasn't Abner's feline companion. He had decided upon the kittens—only the kittens. They had misunderstood our housing arrangement. I still was available. But how could I get that complicated message across to them? Did I have to wait for Abner to drop the other shoe and say something, if he ever did, when he returned?

What was left of my heart felt heavy, as if it had been weighted down by cement and tossed in the river. I wanted a forever home. I liked the Martins and they liked Caryn and me. After my two-and-a-half plus weeks on my own and nearly dying, I knew there was no way, especially at my age, that I was cut out for homelessness and scrounging for meals. I'd been an indoor companion since my kitten-hood eons ago. I certainly didn't want to have to put up with constantly being chased by dogs, cats, and people who hated cats. I sighed. Once fed, bathed, and dried, I attended to the kittens, making sure they were breathing okay and no longer frightened. They all snuggled with me after a harried and tiring day.

The next morning Mr. and Mrs. Martin were huddled together over their square maple breakfast table in deep conversation when the furry five and I wandered in. They looked serious. I rubbed Mrs. Martin's legs, purring loudly. Mrs. Martin said, "Charley, I have sad news. Abner died last night. He had another heart attack. Apparently the smoke inhalation was too much for him after the attacks he had already had." She sniffed, pressed her lips together, and nodded to her husband.

Mr. Martin continued, "Abner didn't have any living relatives so there is no one in his family to take you in. If you'd let us," he reached down beside his wife's chair where I listened attentively and grabbed hold of me to settle me in his lap, "we'd love to have you live here with us—you and the kittens."

Mrs. Martin joined in, her head nodding, "Yes, *please* say you and your family will be ours."

The kittens who had observed me getting attention, started climbing chair- and human legs to get some of their own. I nuzzled Mr. Martin's chest to signify we'd made a contract and sealed the deal with a slurp under his chin. I didn't even mind his facial stubble. Incredibly, in one fell swoop I'd gotten a loving forever home ... and become a "kitty mom"—well, "kitty grandmom" to be more precise—at the same time. It wasn't exactly like having Caryn back but under the circumstances, I couldn't have been happier.

§§§

CHAPTER 6

CASEY

Even though I was considered a rarity, a male calico where only one out of every three thousand calico cats was male, I was little more than an old, pathetic, ragged bag of bones with glittering glacial blue eyes when I was dumped at the Albuquerque Animal Services office on Sunset Gardens. My human companions told the officer on duty that I had been "found." Yeah, sure, they all say that. Nobody asked *me* what had preceded this. They said sanctimoniously they were bringing me in to be put to sleep "because it was the humane thing to do." In my current state of disrepair, I wasn't sure what the truth was any longer ... except I knew I felt rotten.

I had felt rotten for more time than I could remember. It was like having a raging streptococcal infection throughout my body along with unremitting pain. It's odd how pain and prolonged discomfort erase perception of time. Years, months, and days had all run together. I hadn't eaten in some time. I felt too bad to eat but I tried desperately. Still I couldn't. As I lay in my cold cell, I tallied my prospects and options. If this was all life held for me, I might as well die and die now to end this endless suffering—and as Ebenezer Scrooge had put it, "decrease the surplus population." My condition had already dictated that I be put on the Animal Control's death row.

However, the Animal Control Officer who did the intake paperwork that day didn't automatically relegate me to their snuff list. I have no idea why. I'm not sure if she took a liking to me or pity on me ... or she "heard" the messages I was telegraphing. Despite my desire to die and finally get it over with, I had maintained one miniscule glistening speck of hope that things could change for the better though I couldn't imagine how. So I continued shouting at her with every sinuous fiber of my being, that contrary to appearances, I was "salvageable." Of course, that was wishful thinking on my part. I had no idea if my body could be saved and revitalized. To my astonishment she immediately placed a call to a no-kill shelter in the area.

That wasn't what I knew usually happened in the feline equivalent of a death camp. No, frightened feline associates were unceremoniously scooped up by Animal Control, dropped into a minimally comfortable cage to be gassed the next day. Don't get me going about how pounds too often did not look for microchips or check owners' notices of lost cats—even when the owner came to the pound to check and give them a photograph and description.

Sadly, too often the city or county had assigned people ostensibly to "help" those cats who were homeless or running free but either the administrators or workers simply did not give a damn. Cats may not have been worked to near-terminal exhaustion before being gassed, but to me they were captives in a kitty Auschwitz all the same. The number of cats—whether feral, lost, or abandoned—which were summarily "euthanized" daily "because there were so many of them" was mind boggling.

The intake officer called the head of CARMA, Companion Animal Rescue and Medical Assistance, an all-volunteer, no-kill, non-profit in Corrales, NM. She, in turn, immediately reached out to a person in Placitas who fostered and adopted senior cats, no matter what their problem. That female rescuer showed up about forty-five minutes later, cat carrier in hand. The intake officer passionately pleaded my case as the "cat lady" looked me over to see what I needed medically.

"This sweet elderly cat is just hours away from euthanasia," stated the chagrined intake officer. "Can't you help him?"

In spite of my weakened condition and one-foot-in-the-grave, I did my best to be friendly to her. I let her pet me. Whenever I could manage to lift my lead-weight head, I locked my crystalline-blue eyes with hers. Smiling back, she spoke kindly to me as she made a quick inspection of my body. Opening my mouth, she knew instantaneously the primary reason I was skeletal and so ill. The stink of putrefaction slapped her in the face, sharply assaulting her nostrils. My mouth housed nothing but rotted teeth in deep red, oozing abscessed gums. This rescuer signed for me, put me in her carrier, and headed us toward Albuquerque.

Rather than our going directly to her home, which was in a northerly direction, we went to a veterinary clinic in Corrales which was recommended by CARMA. As I waited with my rescuer for the veterinarian, I heard a young person tell her that he had had a cat with such bad breath that he had to sleep with the window open. My rescuer shared with him that bad breath was usually a sign of illness or infection, especially of the mouth. She then calmly asked, "Did you take the cat to a vet to check it out?" The casual response was, "No, besides the cat finally died."

Through the metal cage door of my carrier I could see my rescuer clench her fist as her nostrils flared and jaw clenched but she said nothing further. I figured she regarded this "human" as dumber than a sack of dog hair. Moreover, he was worthy of competing for the annual Darwin Awards for incredibly stupid people doing incredibly stupid things. The Darwin Award was specifically "a salute to the improvement of the human genome by honoring those who accidentally remove themselves from it." I had the impression that my rescuer might have liked to have helped him along in furtherance of his winning it.

It took the veterinarian only a few minutes to manually assess the damage before ordering dental x-rays to determine the extent of the tooth socket and supporting-jaw damage, as well as the existence of roots, if any. All eight of my remaining teeth needed to be extracted. My gums needed to be scraped to remove the purulent dead and dying tissue. And I needed to be on a regimen of an antibiotic ... and lots of pain killers. I didn't have much time to think about how bad it all sounded before I was given a tranquilizer. Fortunately, I wasn't awake when they stuck a tube down my throat to give me some sort of gas anesthesia to knock me out.

The dental surgery was extensive. Ironically, the vet had to only remove seven teeth, instead of eight, because the eighth one fell out into his hand when he touched it. Hours later I was still floating gentle as a cloud, seeing myself lounging on a plump red velvet pillow, being presented with fat mice on silver trays from which to choose for dinner, with each mouse begging to be my "dish of the day."

As I rocked in my anesthesia cradle, I couldn't believe how much better I felt. I was totally pain-free. The surgeon deserved a big, sloppy cat kiss and my undying gratitude. There was no question: he was brilliant, a bloody genius. He had created a medical miracle. He should be hailed as another Albert Schweitzer or at least presented with the Nobel Prize for his professional skills. I'd see he was listed in the *Guinness Book of Records*. I felt no pain whatsoever! What a joy! What an incredible relief. Thank you, thank you, thank you! Then I drifted off again for a while. Recovery from the anesthesia was very slow.

Then I finally woke up. Son of a bitch! I couldn't believe the screaming, head-crushing pain in my mouth that overwhelmed me. If I thought I felt lousy before the surgery, I felt even lousier after. And *that* vet? He was no damned surgeon. He was some worthless back alley butcher. He should have been hung up by his testicles, covered in peanut butter, and attacked by Great Danes! I wanted to kill the bastard with my bare paws.

I was still on an IV drip, but was it for pain? Couldn't be! But if so, someone had forgotten to turn the thing on. I wanted to crawl out of my skin. I couldn't think of anything harsh enough to say. Hey! You clowns! I need some help here ... and I need it NOW! I've been through enough of this crap already. Get on the stick and get me some morphine. Dammit!

Fortunately by the time I was wide awake, they did attach a Fentanyl patch on the shaved spot on my right front leg. It was covered with a piece of that orange crinkly stretch fabric for protection from my gnawing it off (with *what* I might ask) or just coming loose. Usually it is applied six–to–twenty-four hours *prior* to the start of certain surgical procedures, allowing the pain relief medication to reach effective levels in a cat's blood before the surgery actually takes place. The objective was that there wouldn't be any pain after the anesthesia had worn off.

But why the hell hadn't they done it in my case I was demanding to know. Even as the morphine-like patch began mitigating my pain, I was still royally miffed. Later, however, I learned that because of my extremely malnourished condition, my infection-impaired and -weakened heart and body, the vet was concerned about my surviving the surgery if they started the patch early. That modulated my anger a touch. If they had let me know ahead of time, I would have suggested they give me a piece of leather to bite on. Chuckle. But, of course, that wouldn't have helped since now I had nothing to bite with.

When my rescuer came the next day to pick me up, she was told that I would continue to wear the patch for three–to–four days because continuous delivery of pain relief is more effective than periodic administration. I can believe that because I'd seen humans suffering who had to wait for a specific time to get their next slug of pain medication. And by the time they received it, they were already in great pain made worse by their anxiety about getting the pain med in time. It made sense to me to prevent pain rather than alleviate existing pain which takes so much longer. I found out that my recovery from surgery would be much faster if my pain were alleviated. You don't have to be a human doctor to figure that one out. Still, I did appreciate surviving the surgery.

The mantra was that by the end of four days I should be feeling lots better. If not, I should go back to the vet who would put on another patch. You see, civilians weren't supposed to handle this opioid patch. Big whoop-dee-doo. I don't know if the vets were more concerned about humans getting a high from it or just didn't want to be liable for their having access to a controlled substance with no personal prescription. Given the cost of their medical liability insurance, I can understand their caution. So my rescuer, in essence, gave a snappy salute and clicked her heels, shouting out, "Yes, sir."

Even though I was not a biochemist, I was amazed that the vet said to throw the patch down the toilet when it was finished. Down the toilet? Maybe, only if you had a septic tank. But even then, what would that do to the good bacteria in the tank? But if you had city water, disposing of it "down the toilet" sent this potent med into the town's rivers, creeks, or water supply from which we all drink. Do you know how many prescribed powerful chemicals are tossed down the toilet or sink every day and what that does to both humans and animals over time? Whoa! Maybe that accounts for the strange, zombie-like behavior of so many humans.

Anyway, that my pain was being taken care of sounded good to me. At least I was finally feeling a little better. My rescuer would, however, have to monitor me to see if I had any negative reaction to the pain med—you know, vomiting, lethargy, agitation, decrease in appetite, like that. But, come on, there was no way that pain med could have given me any further decrease in the little appetite than I already had.

The clinic put me on a regimen of ten days of an oral antibiotic. This meant my rescuer had to be super-careful in dribbling the liquid into my mouth so that the syringe didn't disturb my laser-cauterized gaping tooth sockets and tender gums. At least I didn't have sutures to drive my tongue crazy. Do you have any idea how huge an empty tooth socket feels to your tongue? Gigantic! That meant I had to make a point of not moving when she slipped the med into my cheek pouch. Her giving me the med also meant she had to be ever-so-gentle and careful in holding my head near my jaw to do it. But by now, I was feeling pretty laid back. The Fentanyl helped. Whee! So if her fingers slipped just a little, I could be cool about it. I'd put up with worse ... LOTS worse.

To keep a close eye on me, she created a place for me in her office where she spent most of her time. I now had a thick foam bed in which to snooze and rest my old bones, a sparkling cat pan with unscented litter, fresh water, and chicken or tuna broth. Crunchy dry food would have to come much later if it came at all. When she wasn't talking with clients on the phone or tapping on a computer keyboard, she was stroking me and talking to me.

I hadn't been there a full day before scarfing down some food sounded like a capital idea. Cautiously, I lapped up the liquid. My dogs, it felt good going down because my mouth no longer hurt. Hopefully that meant that starting to gum soft food wasn't that far in the future—as long as it was as tasty as the liquids.

Even though I went to baby food meats for a little while, it was not long before I was eating regular soft canned meals. Soon I was putting on pounds and re-growing my previously beautiful white coat splattered with blobs of orange and black. I'd been given a new lease on life. I considered saying "a new leash on life" but that was an example of typically bad human humor. Well, at least I felt well enough to be willing to make a bad joke, even if it was a "human" one.

My life had opened up for me like a Graham Thomas rose: a reflection of liquid sunshine, unusually rich, pure yellow that is hard to match, and vigorous upright growth, that boasts fragrance, beauty, and performance. I felt like a blooming flower. I could do just about anything I wanted. I could play with toys, go out for walks in a harness with my rescuer, or lie around comfortably in my new digs.

I fully made my affectionate nature known to her. I was so grateful and happy to become a fully-functioning cat again that I sometimes overwhelmed my new human with rubbing, head bunting, licking, and kissing. I have no doubt she truly appreciated my involving myself in her work by sitting my no-longer-bony rump on her computer keyboard and papers. Of course, there was no way to sufficiently thank my rescuer for all she had done.

Not one to hide my light under a bushel, I have to immodestly state I was turning into a handsome cat again. Months went by all too quickly as I reveled in my new quality life. I savored my tasty meals, treats, lots of active play time, and brushing. My life had become amazing. I was living each and every day to the fullest. I was so grateful. Life was good.

But I couldn't say in all honesty that initially it totally made up for the years of neglect and abuse. As weeks went by, the past faded into the past. It was over and done with. I was no longer suffering with incredible mouth pain, ravaged by blood poisoning, all alone and uncared for, and then abandoned to lie in a cold cage, awaiting chemical finality. Continuing to think about it only made me feel bad and take the edge off my new life. So I stopped. I had been reborn.

With my new incarnation I was experiencing the love, devotion, and respect of a human companion. It was more meaningful than I could ever have imagined. We shared thoughts and feelings frequently. Tomorrow was always a surprise gift, bringing something novel and satisfying. Life was incredible. What more could I ask? Even though my rescuer frequently expected me to pose for photographs to show my blooming, I was in hog heaven. Yes, indeed I was very happy.

Nine month passed. After all that time having enjoyed high-level energy and vigor, I noticed I was beginning to feel a little out of sorts. A sense of fatigue had engulfed me like huge wave. I thought, come on, guys, don't let this be me finally starting to feel "old age." Not now. I'm on a winning streak. Everything has gone so spectacularly well.

Suddenly food that I had rushed to enjoy seemed to hold less interest for me. I was thirsty all the time and beginning to vomit. Fresh catnip which I was orgasmic over no longer stirred my juices. My motivation to take walks around her colorful flower garden, sniffing blossoms, chewing grass, chasing butterflies and moths, and digging under mulch was rapidly dwindling. Batting at a string or chasing a glittery, flashing cat ball across the floor seemed too much trouble. My belly seemed to stick out more in spite of my lack of appetite. I was sleeping more and moving around less.

And my enjoyment of life? It was slipping though my paws, as that soap opera phrased it, "like sands through an hourglass." My companion recognized that a pattern of change was developing in me. I'd gone from enthusiastic to disinterested quickly. That meant heading back in to see the veterinarian ASAP.

Describing my physical, behavioral, and emotional symptoms, she instructed him to do everything necessary to diagnose my problem. He started by shaving a spot on my neck to draw blood for a full-panel of blood tests. Their results showed significant abnormalities in my liver enzymes, bilirubin, and albumin. As my companion already knew from previous cats, that definitely wasn't good. Next were abdominal-chest x-rays. That's when the other cat's paw dropped. The radiographs showed a mass on my liver.

If that wasn't bad enough, the pictures were indistinct. Had I moved when they were taken? Lying on that cold hard glass while someone positioned me just right then snapped the picture was not easy or comfortable. But, no. The translucency which was approaching opacity was from something else. What the fuzziness suggested was that not only was there fluid in my abdomen but also it was not clear fluid.

It wasn't until then that I noticed that my breathing was increasingly requiring more effort. This signaled that the fluid in my chest was pressing on my lungs and impairing my air intake. Of course, these findings required even more tests be done. Distressing thoughts crossed my mind. A mass? That didn't sound good. What about my heart? Was it failing? How about my kidneys? Were they involved? Fudge. Whatever was amiss with my liver, I was willing to put up with more tests *if* it would likely make me feel better again.

My companion and the vet agreed to have a specialist human come to do an ultrasound. I had no idea what that was. When that came to pass early the next morning, the specialist laid me in a blue padded inverted saddle-like structure that was actually pretty comfortable for being on my back. Then he shaved my belly bare, smeared on some cold goop, and ran some sort of gizmo over my abdomen.

He made it pause here, stop there, then repeated the process. As he moved it around, he watched a monitor, clicking various keys on the attached keyboard, as if taking photographs. A quick glance convinced me it would never replace TV or even Mario Brothers. Resigned to do whatever was necessary to get this show on the road, I never said a word throughout this long procedure. I only looked at my companion occasionally.

She looked back, lovingly, reassuringly. However, after having spent one whole hour on having my abdomen "surveyed," I was not the least bit interested in the specialist sticking long, thin needles into my enlarging belly. He referred to it as doing "needle biopsies" to get tissue samples. It was then he announced that on the ultrasound he had found a mass on my urinary bladder as well as on my liver. Consequently, he would do biopsies of both masses. That news didn't make my day.

As he poked, prodded, and stabbed me repeatedly—it didn't really hurt that much, I was determined to stay calm and mature about it all. As I glanced at my companion, I could see she was looking concerned, her face drawn, but trying not to show it. She attempted to smile at me but only her lips curved upward. She was having everything done that she could in order to find out what could make me better. "Better" was looking more and more like wishful thinking. I relied on her judgment but we both sensed things were not going well. She leaned toward my left ear and spoke soothingly about having a special treat when we arrived home, how much she loved me, and how she'd do whatever was necessary to keep me from suffering again. That was comforting.

The specialist told my companion not only that I had two large masses but also that I had an abdomen was full of *bloody* fluid. That's why they couldn't see much on x-rays. To get a specimen of the fluid he then proceeded to use a large syringe, which looked like the proverbial horse needle, to remove some. Then he continued to drain off over 250 milliliters of red fluid to ease pressure on my heart, lungs, and other internal organs. Before that, my lungs had already started to feel heavier and burn as if I were drowning in my own fluids. Of course, lying horizontally on my spine like that was something that definitely was not helping my lungs function properly under the circumstances.

"The source of blood is unknown," he said. "And there's no way it could be determined through ultrasound. That would require exploratory surgery."

Whoa, dude! Hold your horses! Cutting me open to look around, in hopes of discovering the source of the blood that was leaking into my abdomen? And what if they didn't discover the source, then what? Sew me back up? If they did find the source, could they repair it? And what about the two masses already lurking there, continuing to get bigger?

The vet, my companion, and the specialist huddled together to toss this diagnostic football around. Hey, guys! That pigskin you're so cavalierly passing off is my life.

Taking the lead, the specialist stated that the diagnosis undoubtedly was cancer and likely fast-spreading. Even though he was shipping the cells off for laboratory analysis under a microscope, he felt certain my biopsies revealed malignancy. He just didn't know what kind yet. Furthermore, even though he couldn't specifically distinguish any smaller tumors because of the diffuse liquid, he was likewise certain I had a gut full of them. I wanted to challenge him on that. Since he said he couldn't see these so-called "small tumors," how could he assert they were there? But, really, that was totally beside the point. And down deep I knew it.

As a consequence, my options were, to say the least, few. I could have surgery to determine and hopefully repair blood seepage and remove any masses found. I could have chemotherapy or surgery and chemo. Of course, I could also have nothing done. The vet and specialist agreed that *without* surgery or chemo, I had four–to–six months max. Huh? Four–to–six *months*? What exotic material had they been smoking? From the way I felt I knew that was a crock and a half.

My companion looked at me. Her nose was turning pinker. I shouted with my eyes and ear movements that my body already felt as if I had been run over by an Abrams tank. There was no longer any battle to fight. I had already lost it. I definitely didn't want to be opened up so they could muck around, even if they removed any masses they found. Besides, given my current deteriorating physical state, I didn't think I could survive surgery. But if by some miracle I did, I didn't want to spend the rest of my time with my companion recovering from major surgery. I was already in pain and didn't need any more on top of it. Been there and done that, folks. We're talking *quality* of life, not quantity. As far as I was concerned, longer was not necessarily better.

As for chemo, I had heard that it took time for the chemo to take effect. Whatever I had left it wasn't time. Besides, that wouldn't address the bellyful of bloody fluid. I was bleeding internally, perhaps exsanguinating, and getting worse by the hour. My companion blinked back tears, looked up, paused, locked eyes with me, then met the gazes of the vet and technician. Mouth tight, she shook her head "no." She knew there was no way I had four–to–six months irrespective of treatment type. She requested another Fentanyl patch for my increasing discomfort. Thank you. End of discussion.

Back in her office that afternoon she tried to persuade me to have some more tuna juice or chicken bouillon. She dribbled some into my mouth. Encouraged, I lapped it up from the bowl. But the next day I found I couldn't reach for the bowl. My legs felt weak and tingly. They no longer could hold me up. I couldn't stand for more than an instant before I flopped over. As the afternoon wore on, once I'd flopped over, I stayed that way no matter how I tried to get up. She again employed her trusty syringe to drip the liquid into my mouth. Surprisingly, I could no longer taste it.

Things seemed to be changing exponentially. Being able to maneuver myself into and use the litter pan soon became a thing of the past. Seeing my distress, my companion picked me up and carried me into it, holding me upright. Afterward, she cleaned me off and gently placed me on my super-soft bed. This was so undignified, especially for a proud, mature, and worldly-wise cat. As evening approached, I started convulsing. Initially the seizures were more than two hours apart but became more frequent as the night wore on.

Early the next morning she placed a call to the vet to get something to control my seizures. Because she didn't want to stress me further by driving me to the vet, she waited for the return call, never leaving my side. It was comforting how she devoted all her time to care for me, anticipating my every need. She talked softly, stroked my back, and scratched under my chin and around my ears. It helped take the edge off of things. She was eager to get me started on an anti-convulsive and hoped she could get it in injection form.

As the day wore on, she discovered that giving me anything by mouth was problematic. I had started to cough up droplets of water she had slipped into my cheek pouch to help keep my mouth and throat moist. Because of the amount of fluid accumulating in my chest and abdomen already it was recommended that I not receive any sub-cutaneous fluids to hydrate me. My kidneys and heart were already at risk and likely overloaded. It was obvious that if things weren't at least fifty percent better tomorrow, my companion was very probably going to have to say "good-bye" to me. Her nose was again bright pink and her eyes glimmering.

As she kept checking her watch, I lay propped up in her arms, no longer able to swallow. Even if chicken broth—drop by drop— could have quelled my thirst and hunger, I would have choked on it. My companion attached my new Fentanyl patch, which she had convinced the vet to let *her* apply, and just held me gently, soothingly. I couldn't believe how quickly my body was betraying me. I found I no longer had any control my bladder or bowels. I couldn't even gradually move my upper torso around to look at my companion.

With my body now placed into the crook of her arm, she kept my head and chest elevated so I could look at her and breathe more easily. I could see she was conflicted. She tried to smile but her wrinkled brow, down-turned mouth, and damp cheeks betrayed her thoughts. I knew she was torn between giving me all the quality time I could possibly have and not letting me sink into the morass of suffering again.

That incredible "four–to–six–month" prognosis played and replayed in my mind. It was impossible, unthinking, and cruel. Did they really believe what they said? Even if they had meant to say a "four–to–six–*week*" prognosis, did they really feel that was remotely possible, with or without surgery or chemo? The reality, which I grant was extremely hard for me to accept after everything previously, was that there was nothing left for me. There was nothing she or anyone else could do to extend my pain-free, less compromised time on earth.

For almost nine months I had had a good, fun, quality life. I was so grateful. Compared with my near-decade of suffering with unspeakable mouth pain, starvation, being all alone and uncared for, then abandoned, I'd have to say I had sat in the catbird seat for nearly three-quarters of a year. Unlike far too many others, I had had a reprieve, albeit a short reprieve. I had received love and experienced the kind of relationship only a caring human companion could provide. Needless to say, I wouldn't have minded enjoying a few more years of it, but that's another story.

As it approached 1 a.m., I had another seizure, then another, and another. I fixed my fading gaze on her. I told her it was okay. I'd had a great run … all because of her. I'd never forget her and we'd always have that shared love to remember. At that moment an Eckhart Tolle quotation I had once heard came to mind: "You are here to enable the divine purpose of the universe to unfold. That is how important you are." As she cradled me for the last time, I lifted my whiskers up as far as I could, smiled, and thanked her for lovingly helping me to achieve my purpose.

§§§

CHAPTER 7

LUCKY

Through the feline grapevine I had heard that neighborhood and feral cats had discovered a tapas bar in our village on a ridge to the east. The bar was located on a brick porch area under a large overhang which was good for protection from rain, snow, or wind while eating. What awaited anyone who wandered by every morning and dusk was some kind of surprisingly tasty dry cat food in a large Pyrex baking dish along with several dishes of fresh water. Since I had been on my own scrounging for meals only somewhat successfully for what seemed like ages, this sounded like a dream come true. And sure enough, the food and water were there. I'd struck gold.

As I quickly discovered, however, there was a chow line, a queue. That meant I had to bide my time to let the others who had preceded me have their fill first before I could grab a bite. Ah, yes, "grab a bite" was ironic. You see, many cats, dogs, coyotes, and raccoons had already grabbed a bite ... of me ... and not with my blessing. That is, every time I turned around any day some antagonistic beast was chasing me, raking me with their claws, or taking chunks out of my flesh. When dogs could catch me unawares, I became their soccer ball. I don't know why I was their specific target.

Once upon a time I had an attractive, carefully-attended short gray coat and athletically-sculptured flesh on my bones. However, over time, I became the victim of any animal trying to show its superiority or territoriality. My body now was covered with scratches, scars, bleeding wounds of varying depths, and fragrant running abscesses. Because of my increasing ill health and struggle to find food, I was cadaverously thin. My weakened condition, body stink, and unkempt appearance made me the object of human scorn and rejection as well. I was a pariah among both cats and most humans, making my days and nights painful, solitary, and bone-gnawingly lonely.

Surprisingly the human who put out the free food for all of us did not seem repulsed by me. That was a first. Every so often I could see her looking at me through the glass panel to the right of her four-paneled wood front door, two steps above where the food was positioned. Her watching went on for months. I finally not only accepted her observing but also expected it. Slowly over time she opened the front door, talking to me. Of course, I was leery of her intentions.

Even as I delicately stuffed my face, I wondered if she had an ulterior motive for leaving the food for us. At first it had flashed across my mind that she might be another possible enemy. Maybe she was a cat torturer. Maybe she wanted to sell me to a vivisectionist. Maybe, God forbid, she made crush films. I was so jaded about humans that all sorts of crazy improbabilities crossed my mind. To be safe I kept looking up as well as over my shoulder for escape if necessary as I ate.

Then one day she slid into a sitting position on the top brick step. She was still talking to me, inviting me to come near. As afraid as I was, I wanted to approach her—I yearned to approach her. Fear clanged in my ears. Don't do it. People hurt you. Yet a small voice echoed in my head, saying, Yes, do it. You have to trust someone. Not everyone is cruel. Stuck between a rock and the hard place of approach-avoidance behavior, I didn't—I couldn't—approach, even as weeks then months went by.

Over time she had shifted to the lower step and still beckoned me to her. My fear was still arm-wrestling with that small positive voice. Just maybe I could. I could try it out to see what happens. I didn't have to get too close. I could see if she made any questionable moves. Come on, give it a try. You know you really want to. And I really did.

Setting my jaw, I finally took the risk. I inched near to her. She extended her hand at my eye level and held it there. I walked up to it, sniffed, and waited. She gently stroked my head from behind, avoiding my wet wounds. She knew not to put her hand over my head because it would likely feel aggressive and threatening. Her touch was wonderful but I still kept up my guard. What had older and wiser cats always said? Oh, yes, *if a smart cat wants to survive, it could never be entirely certain what a human would try to do to it.* But I didn't want to remain a cynic if it meant continuing to be alone ... and starved for attention.

Every day I came by when the others had finished. I made a special attempt to be there in the late afternoon because that was when she appeared to talk to me, let me approach, and pet my head. I slowly allowed her closer and closer access to me. At times she moved a cloth near my body to dab the ever-present open wounds on my back and sides but I shifted position. There was simply too much discomfort in those areas for her to touch me. Moreover, new wounds were joining old ones. Soon I couldn't keep the dripping of pus-filled blood under control. I was now leaving odiferous trails wherever I moved. And I was walking more slowly these days, even more a victim for single or gang attacks, with no relief in sight.

The next time I arrived she had a towel in her lap. I noshed awhile, warily eying the towel. It didn't bode well. As I crept toward her extended hand, I saw her lift the towel with the other. The moment she raised it, I knew she was going to try to trap me. Fight or flight? Flight, of course! I turned on a slow dime and reversed course, looking back at her, meowing, "How could you? I trusted you! You're just like all the other humans!" She let the towel drop and extended her arms at her sides with palms facing me, shook her head, and made apologetic noises. Then she turned around, opened the front door, and threw the towel inside.

The following day I eased over to her, cocked my head, and looked up to indicate a little petting wouldn't be out of order. I'd given the situation a lot of thought. I was getting weaker every day, my head and body ached, and my limbs felt like lead and wouldn't cooperate with my desires. I was highly unlikely to do well trying to fend off another attack, especially by a raccoon or dog. Moreover, there was no question that my untreated abscesses and blood loss would catch up with me soon ... very soon. I was resigned.

Walking past her up the two brick stairs, I gave her right shoulder, on which was draped a dish towel, a butt with my head. I glanced at the door and wondered if she were getting my message. She whispered, "Are you really ready to go in?" I looked her in the eye then looked at the door again. Reaching slowly into her jacket's left pocket, she removed a pair of latex gloves that she shrugged into. Then she lowered her hands to the sides of my shrunken abdomen. She gripped me with tenderness, avoiding touching the open sores. She couldn't, however, avoid the bacterial exudate oozing down my sides and around my tail. It was time. We both knew it. I couldn't play loner, macho gambling cat any longer. I was down to my last chips. I couldn't afford to bet on my losing hand.

Holding me against the towel which she had now spread across her chest, she opened the door and slipped me onto a thick bath towel which had been snugged into a small space. It was a carrier positioned just inside the foyer. Even though it was time, I felt suspended between anxiety and thankfulness. It had been so many months since I had first presented myself and I was still alive—just barely—because of her—despite my raging septicemia.

The next thing I knew I was at a veterinary clinic. When the vet looked at me, she shook her head, and exclaimed, looking me in the eyes, "I am astonished. You are one amazingly lucky cat to still be alive." Then she looked at my rescuer and said, "I know you will come up with a name for him but given his current tenuous hold on life, I'd name him 'Lucky,' maybe even 'Damned Lucky.'"

She gave me a mild tranquilizer, shaved around all my wounds, flushed them several times with some antiseptic wash, and installed latex drains. Because of the size of the abscesses, she carefully tacked the tubes in place to the abscess tissue edges.

Time passed slowly, awkwardly. Even though I had received a tranquilizer, it was still downright painful but I was unable to do anything about it.

There was no way I was not going to display anything but courage. Cats are not supposed to be wimps or ever display "wimpy" behavior. They're expected by the world at large (that is, "humans") to stoically "take it." You know, you could have had your back leg ripped off in trench warfare with a pack of snarling, slavering canines but you're supposed to dismiss it with, "It's only a flesh wound," and then continue to fight with valor. Yeah, sure. The reality is that cats don't and would never believe such testosterone-coated fecal nonsense.

Well, I take that back a little. I do know a couple of hot-headed, not very bright adrenaline-junkie felines who would. But, in general, we'd analyze the situation in a nanosecond and take off for higher ground. Cats don't sacrifice themselves because it's the so-called "honorable, valorous, or patriotic" thing to do. When we do "it," it's for love, friends, and family, saving those most precious to us from harm. I don't understand humans fighting for the sake of fighting or symbols.

When they were finished with my make-over, I was nearly-hairless, with white-grid markings crisscrossing my torso, and spikey-looking body art rising from my red-rimmed flesh craters. As if I weren't already the epitome of "pure Grunge," they added a stylish plastic Elizabethan collar to prevent my licking, biting, and dislodging the drains. It was clear that lying down, eating, drinking, and using a litter pan were going to be a challenge. Great. That was just what I needed.

To eradicate my full-body infection I had to be given foul-tasting liquid called clindamycin daily for fourteen days. Ptooie! I don't see why it couldn't have been mouse flavored to make it easier to slide down my gullet. After all, the pain med Metacam is supposed to taste like ferret. I wonder who made that determination. How would any human know what ferret tastes like? Or how it would taste to a cat?

However, that wasn't all. In a few days, well before I finished with the antibiotic, I had to go back to the vet to check the wounds, remove the drains, and suture the holes. Unfortunately, when I returned, the vet was chagrinned by the amount of "necrotic tissue"—gross dead skin and flesh—which had to be removed before I could be stitched together. At least she didn't say, "Oops!" Blessedly, I was allowed to sleep through it all.

The results? OMG! John Keats may have written that "A thing of beauty is a joy forever. Its loveliness increases"—and I don't want to contradict a famous English poet—but for a formerly-good-looking cat I was now anything but a "thing of beauty." I looked like a colorful patchwork quilt with many of the cloth pieces missing. Furthermore, I had no doubt my loveliness would not increase, no matter how much skin still had follicles available to regenerate my fur coat. My rescuer told me repeatedly not to worry, that my fur would grow back and cover the scars. Some humans can be such optimists or—more likely—such kindly liars.

For my recovery I was parked in her utility room with the washer, dryer, and wash tub. Despite my soft, padded kitty bed, my litter pan, nutritious food and well water, a window to look out, and lots of human attention, I felt like a prisoner. Adding insult was the fact that I was still wearing the awkward, uncomfortable collar. This kind of isolation doesn't suit any cat but particularly a cat who had wandered most of his life. It was as if I had been treated with Radioactive Iodine for hyperthyroidism which made me off-limits from everyone without a radiation-shielding Hazmat suit for nearly three weeks because I still glowed in the dark, registering rapid clicks on a Geiger counter.

Weeks went by as my wounds slowly healed. I had a white scar on my butt that encircled my tail and abstract drawings on my lower back and sides. Irrespective of what my rescuer expected or wishfully thought, my back was left randomly hairless and diseased appearing, as if I had large spots of permanent ringworm. There was nothing inconspicuous about them. However, given my new state of health, I could finally be introduced to the other felines who resided in the rest of the house.

I admit to being a little shy at first. After all this was their territory. I was "a stranger in a strange land." As I regained my health and strength, I likewise regained my confidence. It occurred to me as I accommodated to the others that had been rescued some time before me that I was still one tough cat. I had survived the worst of the horrors of being an outdoor cat fending for myself and had done it while severely injured and ill. My fellow occupants should, therefore, acknowledge this and show me respect. They didn't have to genuflect or cower. I didn't require a Purple Heart or Medal of Valor. Just give me space and first dibs on treats and scritches. Why shouldn't I be the new alpha cat? Of course, I knew the pecking order had already been established. But still ...

Then I met Rambo. All twenty-seven pounds of long black fur, muscle, and more than a little adipose tissue, he was truly the alpha cat. He took no crap from anyone, except his rescuer. He swaggered when he walked, although it could have been from continually-shifting fat rather than from arrogance. Typically, he shoved himself through a crowd to get a piece of human-proffered smoked turkey. He pushed cats away from their dry and canned food dishes so he could check out what they had received and determine if it were better than what he had. Given his girth, it was obvious he always managed to be first at the trough.

From his personality I could tell he had emotional problems from kitten-hood. As it turned out, he had been dumped in a shelter's mailbox, desperately ill with three types of bacterial diarrhea. No one knew what had happened before he was abandoned, but he obviously had needs that weren't being met to his satisfaction. There was something pathetic about him. I had heard that as a youngster, he also would chew on other cats' whiskers whenever he could. His behavior was more than a little annoying to those left with whisker stubble because it significantly reduced the use of their vital tactile sensory organs.

Because I was one-third of Rambo's weight, I had no desire to do battle with him when he became pushy. Besides, as a result of my past life, I was inclined to be a pacifist. So instead of playing the game by Rambo's rules, I decided to use my cunning, superior jumping ability, and newly adopted feline-human communication skills to get what I wanted. As a result, I always beat him onto the kitchen sink so my companion could turn the water tap on for me. Slurping tap-fresh water was my treat. I spoke to my human to suggest playtime or petting or cuddling. And I showed appreciation for her desired response.

I discovered that Rambo and I were alike in one respect but totally different in others. We both were Human-Whisperers but he hadn't as yet become aware of and smart about how to use his natural skills to develop a good relationship with his human. He hadn't as yet tumbled to the realization that working with his human was much more advantageous—more satisfying and gratifying—than making sure all eyes and attention were focused on his display of aggressiveness.

Becoming aware of and smart about developing a good relationship with a human was something I had grudgingly come late to. If I hadn't recognized and applied my Human-Whispering skills, I might have died. Yep, in fact, I had almost let myself die because I was too wracked with fear to step back to analyze objectively what the situation required, what I needed to do that would be most beneficial to me. I almost didn't communicate with and listen to my human about the life and death circumstance facing me. I almost didn't accomplish the life-saving change. Fortunately, most cats are not like Rambo and me in that they don't need a metaphorical two-by-four to the back of their skulls to get their act together and use their Human-Whispering. Oh, and guess who is *now* the first one to enjoy those lip-smacking smoked turkey treats. You got it.

§§§

CHAPTER 8

HARRY

Before my human companions divorced, I thought my name was "Kitty Dammit." Okay, that's an old human joke, but things were tense and became much more intense before they signed the legal papers that separated them permanently. I had started out as an adopted kitten, with long pure white hair, black-outlined green eyes, and a tail that promised to be as spectacular as a pampas grass panicle. I had been chosen by the female half of the unit to be their forever companion. The name assigned to me back then when things were all lovey-dovey between them was "Harry." They both interacted with me then but I was more her cat then his.

When the big split occurred, twelve years later—a split so tumultuous that it echoed reminders of the movie "The War of the Roses"—he demanded to have me. This puzzled me. I knew for a fact this desire to have custody of me wasn't a consequence of his great love for me. I was *her* cat. I suspected I had become a pawn in the game between them. Somehow he got custody. I was astonished. Didn't she fight for me? I wish I knew. Since I wasn't privy to all the particulars of the legal wrangling and how these decisions were made, I was at a loss as to why she hadn't kept me. We were best buds. Despite his overarching anger, I hoped that he and I could manage to be civil to one another and get along.

Each morning before the sun rose, he pushed me out the front door, put a half-cup of dry food and water on the front porch, and didn't invite me back in until it was dark, after he returned from work at a local bank. I was pretty much on my own all day to wander the neighborhood and beyond to seek food and attention in other locations. I was becoming well known as I traversed the scrub, pricky pear and cholla cactus, and rocky outcroppings of the surrounding area. Wandering this type of landscape could be hazardous aside from encountering rattlesnakes and scorpions. More than once I stepped on a cactus spine, a sharp piece of obsidian, or slipped off a rock face, twisting an appendage. I found that my superb balance and athleticism were no match for these natural dangers.

As I explored in ever-widening circles away from my dwelling, I found it was better to avoid, whenever possible, the two-lane road that paralleled my territory. Speeds were nearly always in excess of what safety required. As a result, more than a few burrowing rock squirrels had met their end trying to cross it. Disemboweled carcasses littered the asphalt off Copper Basin Road. Sometimes I wondered if my human wanted me to have a similar fate. I don't know. Maybe I was judging him too harshly. He wasn't exactly cruel to me, just maybe a bit too laissez-faire for my sense of what a cat-human relationship should be.

However, the other side of the road called to me, like Sirens calling to sailors. Only this call wasn't to my doom. It rose from the surface up the ridge. One place I could see was about fifty feet back from the road, through pine trees, on the way to Granite Peak. It had tiers of railroad ties for native plantings below a three-foot rock wall that surrounded the house on two sides. I had to see what was beyond the wall.

Inside the wall was not a disappointment. There displayed was a riot of colors. Abundant were single- and complex-petaled roses, blue and green chamisa, pink and tangerine mallow, valerian, yellow achillea, terra cotta chrysanthemums, blue Russian sage, purple catmint, and magenta dianthus. There was a front deck of wood, painted silver green like the house, which jutted out, cantilevered over junipers and pinons below. On it was stationed a long, low glass dish of dry, mixed-flavors cat chow and a dish wash basin full of fresh water. This was like a resort where I could lounge and re-energize between trips. This became my daily destination.

Frequently in the early evening as I sat on the stone wall I saw a new female human there who extended a friendly welcome to me. I've always been a glass-half-full kind of cat. Unless I have reason to distrust the human, I tend to stay open to positive interactions. Of course, that isn't to say I'm unwary. No, I monitor and analyze my environment then act upon that. When she offered to pet me, my ESP-like antennae reception, perhaps referred to as "intuition" by humans, told me this was okay.

And it was better than okay. She really knew how to make a cat feel like dancing. She scratched my neck, my cheeks, under my chin, around my ears, and at the top of my tail which made me get all squinty-eyed, forcing me to lick like crazy. Then she'd use long petting strokes on my back and belly. She smoothed my long hair. Completely relaxed and feeling cared for, I wanted to tell her I was hers, all hers, heart and soul. I hadn't experienced this kind of attention since before my own female human left.

After seeing her nearly every day for a month, I missed catching her several days running. I was moving more slowly to get there. When I saw her again, she stared at me with her mouth agape. I knew why. I had stepped on a sharp rock or piece of glass that left a gash. It had not been tended to by my male human over the weeks that followed the injury. Now my back right leg was swollen and the skin under my white fur was purplish red, causing me to limp. When she examined me, she discovered the laceration on my foot which had abscessed and developed into blood poisoning. It hurt to walk but not enough to prevent my returning for food and her company. I let her wrap a towel around me, pick me up, and take me to her vet. The caring attention was wonderful.

The vet took one look at my leg and foot and recommended that my rescuer keep me inside and inactive for ten days as she gave me the antibiotic Clavamox twice a day by mouth and soaked my leg in warm salty water four times a day. Clavamox pretends to have flavors added that cats enjoy. I don't know whose opinions they sought in their marketing research, but it wasn't cats'. My rescuer wrinkled her nose, stating that she thought it smelled like some chemical trying to impersonate bananas. It didn't taste like anything I'd want in my mouth, thank you.

Her sun-drenched utility room became my hospital room. There she had placed a folded blanket on the washing machine as a bed, food and water on the clothes dryer beside it. If I say so myself, I was incredibly patient and tolerant of all she I had to do. That repeated soaking my leg in warm salt water made my fur wet and my skin surface sticky. I wasn't thrilled with either resulting state. However, her actions spelled out a real concern about my health and welfare which I appreciated. So I licked her hand every time she finished the soaking. Or maybe I was motivated by the salt on her skin. Who knows but I know she and I felt closer as a consequence.

By the time the ten days had elapsed, the leg swelling and discoloration were gone. It occurred to me I could get used to this kind of attention. Before I could leave, she tried to locate my male human. Going door to door down Angelita Drive in the old development and along Copper Basin Road, she spoke with neighbors or left them notes about finding me and tending to my health needs. She asked that my human to call her so she could return me to him. Days passed. I wondered if he would call. Maybe he wouldn't. Maybe that was encouraging.

During the time of my treatment, no flyers had appeared on telephone poles, mailboxes, or front gates announcing a missing cat. This had distressed my rescuer. Did this person know or care? I wondered the same thing. One would hope that if he had gone away for a few days, he would have assigned someone to care for me. If so, this person would have missed me, found the notice of my whereabouts, called my rescuer, or passed along the information to my male human when he returned. After my rescuer had taken her note around to all the houses in the area, the days sped by. I was enjoying my hotel stay with my new companion and trying not to think about his possibly calling. Would he respond? Part of me hoped not. Then on the fifth day after her note, he did call. Since I had finished my treatment, my rescuer drove me the half-mile to my home.

97

My male human, who always managed to seem pleasant enough even a little charming, in social gatherings, appeared stoic about my disappearance. My rescuer expected to see some sign of caring anxiety about my health. She didn't hear any enthusiastic or relieved response, like "Oh, there you are! Let me look at your poor foot. I'm so glad you're back safe and sound." The look on my rescuer's face spoke volumes. It was one of disappointment and gathering concern. My male human didn't seem particularly happy to see me. From their interaction, I suspected my rescuer wasn't exactly thrilled about having brought me back.

However, she explained in detail what the vet had said about the problem and what had been done for treatment. It was his cat so he really ought to know all that had transpired. Because of the location of the wound she pointed out there was increased vulnerability for recurrence of the infection. Furthermore, she emphasized the vet's recommendation that I be monitored for a week to ten days. In reality, I should no longer be allowed to go outside. He nodded in response.

She ended their meeting stating she wasn't asking him for reimbursement for vet services. Somewhat unconvincingly, he then did offer to reimburse her. No. She said she hadn't done it for him; she had done it for me. She wasn't about to acquiesce. My male human gave her a perfunctory nod and thanked her. I could tell as she said good-bye that her intuition told her something was truly amiss with his and my relationship. The next day—which was no big surprise to me—I was outside, roaming. When I arrived in my rescuer's yard again and she saw me, she pinched her lips, narrowed her eyes, and muttered to herself.

Four weeks passed before I was limping badly again. My right back leg was once again swollen. Fortunately, this infection was not yet as bad as it had been before. When my rescuer saw me, she looked annoyed. She made it clear that she was not angry with me as she gently examined my leg. Placed in a cat carrier and settled in the front passenger seat of her red Volkswagen Rabbit, I was driven back to the vet.

As much as my leg hurt, I was enjoying her active compassion. This time the vet wanted x-rays as well as a blood sample. The films revealed that my foot likely had a bone inflammation. I was put on clindamycin again for ten days with frequent salt-water soaking. Her utility room was looking even cozier than I had remembered it.

Even though I was gone another ten days, my rescuer received no word from my male companion inquiring about me. She had chosen not to contact him, wondering if he would contact her now that he likely knew where I was. When the primary infection cleared, she debated whether to return me to him before I was treated with a secondary bone inflammation medication for another week. Against her better judgment, she returned me again to my male human.

This time she handed him the bone inflammation medication with directions for its use. Of course, this came with the requirement that he keep me off my foot for as long as possible—at least a week. I was definitely *not* to be allowed outside during that time. He nodded and took me back without saying anything. Biting the inside of her cheek, my rescuer looked conflicted. I could see she suddenly realized she had made a large error in bringing me back so soon. Carefully, she suggested that she would be happy to take care of me for him since I needed more treatment. "Oh, no," he responded with an edge in his voice. "I've had this cat since it was a kitten." I wasn't sure what that had to do with me or the price of wheat in the south of France but it ended the conversation.

And the next day—surprise or surprises!—he hurriedly let me out first thing to wander around without having given me the new antibiotic my rescuer had handed over to him. Did he forget? This reminded me of what philosopher George Santayana was supposed to have said, "Those who cannot remember the past are condemned to repeat it." Only in this case—forgive my being judgmental—I don't think it was a matter of "remembering." I just think he didn't give a rat's derriére about me.

What followed not having the bone inflammation medication was not unexpected. That mysterious infection continued to brew inside my body. But while I felt reasonably chipper, I indulged in another month of fun visits to my rescuer's yard. She and I were learning what we liked to do together. Mostly we'd walk around her property or sit side by side on her deck to watch the blazing red sunsets or the phenomenon of turkey vultures flying overhead in moving gyres across the sky. I was very comfortable here. I truly felt I belonged.

And then the problem recurred. Golly, who'd have guessed? I slowly arrived at my rescuer's door with my back leg swollen and purple with infection. When she saw me, she gritted her teeth. This situation was more than one just annoyance and expense. It was at the very least one of neglect and cruelty. We were off to the vet … again. The vet, who I'm sure, thought I was really *her* cat, was astonished and confused by this repetition. My rescuer felt not only guilty and embarrassed but also very angry.

As per usual, I was prescribed an antibiotic, a different one this time, and scheduled for warm-water soaking four times a day. By now I looked most fondly on the utility room. It was becoming my home away from home with its freshly laundered, fluffy baby-blue blanket. If I'd had my druthers, I would not have left, ever.

By the end of ten days, my rescuer—and by now I thought of her as *my* companion-friend—grumbled about releasing me. She talked with me about it, "I don't want you to go home. I worry that because we haven't found the underlying reason for these dangerous infections they'll keep happening." Under her breath, she muttered, "And somebody who should be concerned and on top of this isn't helping one bit. On the contrary."

Grudgingly she took me back home but dropped me off on the front porch. I could tell she didn't want to see my male human again. If the expression on her face and the obvious tension in her body were any indication, she was afraid she might say what she was thinking to him, or worse, be sent to jail for assault and battery.

As the panoply of different blossoming flowers rolled on, I continued to reappear daily in her yard to be showered with affection when we connected. She fed me tasty treats, brushed me, commented on how snowflake-beautiful I was, and kept an eye out for any manifestation of my condition. Strangely, my ill health seemed to be on a lunar calendar. There had been approximately thirty days between each vet appointment. And now it was time again. Sadly my body didn't disappoint.

I presented myself to my companion-friend hardly able to walk. Once again the vet said I was to rent my rescuer's utility room for bed and board for ten days. Even after finishing the new antibiotic and soakings, I still was vulnerable. This time after I finished my therapeutic regimen, my rescuer simply let me loose in her yard to return "home" on my own. She told me in confidence that she did not want me to go. And if I didn't want to return to my male companion, I had a standing offer of a permanent home with her.

Conflicted, she worried about the possible legal problem of her simply keeping me—and keeping me safe. I was legally his "property" if he chose to object—and he'd already said "no" to her taking me. As morally reprehensible as it would be, he could charge her with "theft." Wasn't it just as morally reprehensible what he was doing to me by disregarding the vet's recommendation?

Another thirty days later I literally dragged myself into her yard. My long thick hair hid nothing. My right back leg was balloon-like, deep, purple, oozing pus, and stinking of dying infected tissue. If I had thought I had seen my companion-friend really angry before, I was wrong. She was, to put it charitably, furious. She looked as if she could kill, if given half a chance, maybe even doing it slowly—shooting one part of his body at a time, starting with his knees, purposely missing vital organs—for the fullest, longest-lasting effect.

For the fifth time, the vet saw me as an emergency. This leg problem had become a puzzle he desperately wanted to solve. Instead of the required ten days this time, the vet said I was to rent my rescuer's utility room for bed and board for two-plus weeks. Even after finishing the new antibiotic and soakings, I was still vulnerable. I should definitely *not* go outside.

So what was going to happen next? The real question was how many more times would my male companion allow me to go through this before my rescuer could no longer act in time and I had to have my leg amputated, or I simply died along the side of the road in my travels? Was this abuse? My companion-friend thought so in spades. Did he care? I didn't think so. Was he just hoping that I *would* crawl away and die? It was hard to think otherwise.

The reality staring me in the face was that if my companion-friend hadn't been around, I very likely would have been dead now, five times over. I was too young and had too much ahead of me to, euphemistically, "go over the Rainbow Bridge" for something that could have been prevented or easily resolved after the first incidence.

Once I was through my treatment, my companion-friend regretfully had to go out of town for several days to present at a business-related conference so she asked a friend and cat sitter to care for me. I felt I could have stayed at my companion-friend's house alone with several days of food, water, and, of course, fresh litter in my litter pan. But she wasn't comfortable with that. According to her, too many unforeseen things could happen in her absence, like accidents, my getting sick again, a water pipe bursting, or a wire shorting starting a fire. Instead, her friend would come in twice a day to check on me, refill my water and dry food dishes, de-divot my litter pan, and play with me. I was so much happier not having to stay at her friend's house which would, no doubt, have been stressful because of the new person, travel, and new environment.

When my companion-friend returned home, she discovered there had been no phone messages, e-mail, or snail mail from my male human, inquiring about me. Because I had been away from male human's home for over twenty days altogether, she checked the neighborhood for flyers. Nothing. She also contacted the animal control and the local veterinarian to see if anyone had reported me missing. Nope. It was disheartening that he cared so little. Maybe he was glad someone else was caring for me. The situation reminded me of "Don't let the door hit you in the butt on the way out."

I tried not to think about it. Even though I was delighted to be with my companion-friend, occasionally I'd recall that my male human never once contacted her about me … other than after my rescuer's initial note. He had contacted her then. But the more I thought about it the more I realized that he had *had* to respond then. After all, my rescuer had scoured the neighborhood, searching for him, knocking on his neighbors' doors, leaving notes of urgency, alerting every one of my illness situation. Since he always let me run, everyone in the area knew me and to whom I "belonged." He didn't want them contacting him or questioning him about me.

It was obvious to me that he responded the first time only to keep up appearances with those around him and to save face. When there were no more notes being circulated about me specifically directed at him, no one would know of my quasi-abandoned situation. He had nothing to worry about, except that my companion-friend would continue to return me to the scene of the crime.

Being erased from my memory, he was quickly relegated to the past. I was now living in the present. This was where I wanted to be. This is where I was meant to be. I was now where I was loved and appreciated and treated like a valued member of the family. On top of it all, I was where I received great catnip!

§§§

CHAPTER 9

GEORGE

They tell me I had a history before I was dropped off at an animal shelter but in all honesty I don't remember it. Or maybe I don't want to remember it. Is that amnesia or repression? Who can say? I am a five-year-old adult Maine Coon cat, sociable and gentle, with a large, solid, muscular body and a silky flowing coat with tabby markings. My eyes, one of my outstanding features, are large, luminous green and delicately outlined in charcoal brown. They hug your heart. From the little black tufts on my ear tips to the fullest, fluffiest tail imaginable, I am one memorable cat.

One hypothesis about my breed has to do with how my lineage arrived in Maine to become the State Cat. It has to do with Marie Antoinette who was Queen of France. The story goes that before she was executed for more than her affirmation "Let them eat cake," she tried to escape by ship to America. While she managed to load her six favorite Turkish Angora cats on board, her execution in 1793 interfered with her leaving as well. So her cats arrived in Wiscasset, Maine, which then bred with short-haired breeds there, and developed into the spectacularly handsome cat you see today. I kind of like that association with royalty.

Another hypothesis, one that's far more likely but less dramatic, is that an English seafarer, Captain Charles Coon, kept long-haired cats aboard his ships. When Coon's ship anchored in Maine and other New England ports, his cats left the ship and mated with the local free-roaming felines. When beautiful long-haired kittens resulted locally, they tended to be referred to as "Coon's cats."

And I am without question a gorgeous cat. But adoptable? Not bloody likely.

You see, I'm disabled. And to put it most accurately, most people aren't interested in a gimp cat. No, I wasn't born this way. Somewhere in my deep, dark past I had lost all but barely four inches of my legs on the left side. Accident to be sure but I don't know how it happened. As a result, I have two normal legs on the right and two leg stumps on left. I can't help thinking it had something to do with a vehicle or large machinery of some sort.

As you might imagine my locomotion is difficult. It's not only because of the stump-lopsidedness but also because I have to walk on skin-covered amputations with nothing like paws or pads to protect the tender bone end. I can almost, not quite, use my front left leg. My back left leg, however, is, for all intents and purposes, useless. Despite its dysfunction, I still try to scratch my neck with that phantom foot. You know how some behaviors are reflexive. That's very frustrating.

This strange disability makes my gait precariously wobbly and my movement generally slow. Furthermore, just to frost the cake, it doesn't even make me a prospect for some kind of wheeled kitty cart, like paralyzed or double-amputee dogs or pigs might be strapped into. And I've seen those critters really move out. Smooth.

My days at the Socorro shelter were numbered. Even though I was still a youngster, there were just too many rescued cats that weren't disabled and were adoptable, except, of course, for elderly, chronically ill, or black cats. Unfortunately it didn't matter to potential adopters that I could melt their hearts in an instant with my tender look, that I waved my good paw to reach out to them, or how artistic my markings were … once they had seen all of my legs. As a result of my disability, I spent most of my time lying on my side in my cage because I couldn't stand up for more than a few seconds at a time unless I started "walking." When I walked, I hobbled, flopping down quickly onto my side when I stopped. I surely didn't dazzle them with my fancy footwork.

Yet this Saturday the gods had shown their faces upon me because someone finally displayed more than a passing interest in me. I stared at her, got her attention, and told her what a wonderful, loving big ball of fur I was. And like a special bargain I wouldn't be available for long. I might be a little awkward but I would make her life even better. By golly, she was truly receptive and scooped me up just in time. My Harley-Davidson purr of joy echoed around the room.

I couldn't quite believe it had happened—we had connected and bonded. But I could tell from her body language that this one was determined that I could have and deserved to have a quality life. But as I quickly discovered, she was really an employee of the shelter who was going to transport me to a rescuer who would care for me. My rescuer knew that the shelter where I temporarily resided was overwhelmed with fully functioning cats and kittens. The shelter itself had to take a practical, more efficacious but less humane position in focusing on those who were most likely to succeed at adoption.

As a result, those of us who weren't likely to be placed were scheduled to go on the scrap pile sooner or later. I found the idea of being relegated to becoming compost simply because of my aesthetically-displeasing left stumps totally unacceptable. But at least they weren't going to send us "undesirables" to certain Asian countries to be skinned alive and then made into stew meat and fur covers for stuffed animal toys.

But I digress. Back to my dear rescuer: As I said, my initial rescuer's role was only to save me from execution but not to keep me with her forever. I hadn't understood that when she whisked me away from a pentobarbital injection or—heaven forbid—a full-blown-panic-suffocation from carbon monoxide gassing, decompression to prevent breathing, or electrocution. I didn't know what this shelter used but hoped for the sake of the animals they would be "humanely eliminated," not by something so torturous.

So I was shuttled about, so to speak, feeling a little disconcerted. This game of what appeared to be musical rescuers was at first confusing then depressing. But while the first one was nice, the second one, named Vicky, went out of her way to make me a part of her animal family. She talked to me and gave me loads of attention. In exchange I sat on her lap, gazed soulfully into her eyes, and provided my turbo-jet engine-grade purr for which I am justifiably famous. She liked me. She really liked me.

Things were starting out well. I had my own room and lots of tasty food but I needed to get out, to explore the place that was to be my permanent home. I mean, once you've circumnavigated the bed and determined you can't leap onto the dresser, what else is there? You're still salivating for attempting the stairs, peeking into closets, and seeing what's been dropped onto the kitchen floor—*your* territory—that might be tasty.

As it turned out, releasing me to wander created a problem with the rescuer's already-present feline companion. He had his tail in a twist. Maybe it was because I was invading his territory. Maybe he didn't like my bubbly personality or to-die-for coat. Maybe I was getting too much attention which he felt left less for him. Maybe he was put off by the strangeness of my disabled behavior. Or maybe it was because he was Feline Immunodeficiency Virus (FIV) positive which includes behavior change once he starts to show clinical symptoms.

Whatever it may have been singly or in combination, as a result, he growled and hissed at me whenever she let me out of my room. Often he'd leap out at me from behind the door to their master bedroom, limbs thrashing. I'd invariably flop over in the rush to get away and end up being paw-slapped silly, receiving a bloodied face for my efforts more often than not.

Vicky kept me for about three months, trying to find an acceptable solution. It was apparent she couldn't let me out without her own cat going kitty bonkers, fur raised, and being in a snit all the time: "If you loved me, really loved me, you wouldn't give that intruder the time of day." Consequently, I was relegated to my room with the door shut ... period. Sometimes she took me into a larger room without a bed in which to play with me. During our assignations, her jealous pal sat outside the door, scratching and yowling. That took more of the bloom off the rose for being in a loving home. It was more like a battleground. I didn't know what to do about it but wanted to do something.

Because I'm not a wallflower when it comes to making my wishes known, I became very vocal. Like, "Hey, guys, how about letting me out of here. I'm not some poor relation you hide in the closet. You invited me here. I want to make this my home too." Between her cat lurking outside my door, chortling at my isolation and constantly suggesting to her that I had no place there and should leave, she decided for everyone's peace of mind I should live elsewhere. I felt bad for Vicky and I felt bad for me. If her cat had only co-operated, I could have stayed there forever, even with her two huge dogs, and had run of the house. But he didn't co-operate.

At that point she diligently searched for a true permanent home for me, contacting other rescuers, asking for recommendations. I was beginning to feel like an old garment— you know, like an old shoe that pinches slightly but because it is attractive and still has some wear it is too valuable to throw away, but not valuable enough to keep it yourself and wear it. Don't get me wrong. I didn't begrudge her actions. My presence was creating a big problem for her. She had her other long-time animal companions and her peace of mind to consider as well as my happiness.

Eventually she heard of a human who took in and cared for disabled, chronically ill, and elderly cats. Though she never described her, I was trying to imagine someone who took in old cats. I figured she had to be old like her cats, stooped with arthritis, barely able to get around. Maybe she was even the stereotype of the "crazy cat lady," someone brain-dead but with good intentions, collecting more and more homeless cats but not able to care for those she had. Lordy! Maybe she was a hoarder. But would Vicky do that to me? I was sure she wouldn't.

That thought did frighten me however. Picturing myself being warehoused with lots of enfeebled and sick felines, I could imagine dead cat carcasses lying around or stacked against a wall. Yeech. I felt my stress level increase. I could envision rows of cages or everyone roaming around aimlessly, no one ever receiving any personal attention except at feeding time, if she remembered. Of course, cat pans would be piled high with urine-caked litter and feces, begging to be cleaned.

But, no, this was ridiculous. My rescuer Vicky would never send me into that kind of situation. She would be very careful to find someone caring and responsible. I was getting upset over nothing. Still, I had been incredibly lucky twice. Was it possible I could be lucky a third time? The odds seemed against me. But, irrespective, there was no way Vicky and I could continue to put up with my current situation.

The "old, crazy cat lady" agreed to come by to meet me one evening. What a surprise! Okay, I have to admit I was wrong, at least about her being old or crazy-looking or a likely hoarder. She looked middle-aged and normal. The first thing she did was talk to me gently and ask me what I wanted. I told her I needed to be treated like a regular cat, respected, and loved. I needed to be allowed to move around as I chose to discover my own territory. I intuited she heard my answers.

Then she asked for a list from Vicky of all the things I liked, didn't like, needed, and any medical history she had on me. After the not so old, not so crazy cat lady assured me she could provide what I wanted and needed, she ended the visit by finding all my "laffin' places." Those are all the delicious spots where I loved to be scratched and petted. Having my tummy rubbed was the ultimate sweetness. Her having known ahead of time it would work out, she had brought a carrier to take me home right then and there.

When I arrived, what a relief! It was just a clean, neat-looking house appearing the way you'd expect a regular residence to look. There were no rows of cages. Nary a cage to be seen, although there were a couple of open cat carriers for those who wanted to relax in a small, confined, private space they could call their own. Cats were wandering everywhere from room to room around the house, presumably with few restrictions. That was a good sign.

While some cats may have been old, they were not enfeebled by any stretch of the imagination. If they were sick, they didn't show it. I did see a shelf with lots of medications and a printed schedule next to it on the wall. Amazingly some of my new associates were blind, partially-paralyzed, brain-damaged, or missing a foot but they all navigated without difficulty and made their presence known. I guessed I wasn't going to be out of place after all.

Of course, my arrival wasn't exactly greeted with trumpets and flourishes. No cat presented me with the key to the city or to the front door. When we entered the house, they visibly displayed displeasure as if they weren't exactly ecstatic, as in "oh, for joy, another cat," having me join them. They sniffed and walked away, almost as if I were last week's garbage. I loudly protested, matching their territorial behavior. I let them know I didn't ask to be here to be treated like this. But if they continued with their treatment of me, I would be a force to be reckoned with. George was no wimp that they could push around. You bet. I was ready for bear if it came to that. But, of course, it didn't. I knew better but the stress had gotten to me. We all were posturing, the same way humans do, but without humans' hidden intentions. That's why I like cats more than most humans.

Still ... why, oh, why couldn't I have been placed with someone who had no other cats? I mean it would not have been a "strain" to be the only cat and the center of attention. I surely could have tolerated it. Now I was back to yowling to be heard above the madding crowd. Even though yowling had worked before to help change my environment, it didn't look as if it would this time. There was too much competition. Hey, it didn't hurt to try. Slowly my new rescuer introduced me to each of the others individually and as a group. It wasn't quite as bad as I had anticipated. Yet I still felt compelled to meow a lot to make myself noticed as a significant presence above the din.

As for my being simply left to my own devices, my new human apparently had no intention of letting that happen. Experience told her that I was likely to lie around, playing "victim," feeling sorry for myself as an outsider, and getting fat. Extra weight would not have been a benefit to walking with my stumpy legs. So she took special interest in stimulating me into action with flying toys and catnip. Actually I wasn't all that interested in or happy lying around like a large lump of splendiferous fur anyway. So I began to take advantage of the exercise. It not only gave me individual attention but also allowed me to participate in group play.

But group play wasn't like touch football with the Kennedy clan. I was slow and awkward. I messed up the game. Consequently, I was left in their dust as we all chased the colorful knotted string around the rooms. If only my front left leg touched the ground and my left rear did more than swing back and forth like a pendulum. If only my back leg as it tried to contribute to my rhythmic forward movement didn't put a lot of strain on my back.

Concerned, my new human talked with me about it. Would I be interested in having some kind of prostheses for my left leg stumps? She didn't know if I'd be a candidate for them because of the length of my stumps. But if so, maybe they could take the strain off my back. And even better, they could help me walk more comfortably, and, maybe, eventually run. That seemed like a pipe dream.

My new human discovered that having prostheses for me was mostly castles in the air. After a lot of research and contacting those who provided this help for animals, such as OrthoPets, she learned that my left legs were too short for prostheses. At under four-inches-long each, they were not long enough to hold the contraptions in place to help me balance and walk efficiently and effectively. That had been a really nice thought though. Yet I'd gotten along for a longtime with my disability. Besides, wearing prostheses on both legs would probably have been a bummer with me wanting to shake them off. Okay, maybe that was just sour grapes.

After about a month, my new human took me outside into her garden so I could explore and stretch my muscles even more. Ah, exercise in the fresh air. The paths in the garden were terra cotta-colored sandstone on which I could gain some purchase in my pursuits. But in between the large slabs was small, sunburst-colored gravel which hurt my tender bone ends. While I moved around slowly, I found I actually could cover some ground when motivated. That was demonstrated when I was burrowing under the stems and long leaves of a profusely-blooming red Jupiter's Beard and discovered ... to my chagrin ... I wasn't alone.

It was night of the living dead! I had come face to face with a snake. What kind of snake? Rattler? Garden snake? Bull snake? Gopher or Rat snake? Who knew? Who cared? I moved out of there as if my tail had been torched. Scrambling, I backpedaled about eleven feet, out of harm's way. My new human raced over to see if I had been attacked. Well, only my dignity. But that was bad enough. How humiliating!

Searching, she found no snake. I suspect our encounter scared the pooh out of both of us as we scuttled in opposite directions. After that, I daydreamed: If only I had had all four appendages intact, I would have slain this dragon, ridding the kingdom of this vicious, populace-threatening beast. But having only a right front paw for my weapon and no leverage, well, that called for plan B. Plan B called for simply getting the hell out of there. I would forget worrying about avoiding public scrutiny and embarrassment. Besides, in doing so I was charitably *letting* the snake continue to do its job of ridding the yard, and possibly the house, of "plague-infected mice."

From then on whenever my new human took me out, if I hopped toward any plant that could hide a snake, she trotted over to check it out before I settled underneath it. I really liked the Jupiter's Beard. But the blue-flowered catmint that the bees ravaged for nectar was even better. I just pushed those busy-buzzers aside so I could roll in its seductive narcotizing scent. Even when my stumps felt they were being tenderized by the wear and tear, I loved being outside.

Despite my inability to wear prostheses, my new human tried make-shift pads and small booties for me merely to protect my leg ends. She actually tried to use duct tape to hold them in place to see if such paw protectors could work. Of course, the sticky tape on the fur just above my stumps irritated me beyond all tolerance. As a result, I spent more time trying to jettison them than to move around with them. As much as she didn't want to, she got the message and finally gave up on them. Of course, then she had to use alcohol to get the adhesive off my lower stumps, as well as shave off some residually-matted fur. No good deed goes unpunished.

Still she took me out daily. I had only to demonstrate how I really lusted being at one with Nature in spite of my stumps. Anytime she needed a reminder, I flopped against the front door and loudly sang an old cat sea shanty, reminiscent of my probable breed's origin.

As I gained more confidence in my place here and in what my more athletic body could do, I had an experience that will always remain my crowning achievement. My new human and I were making trips down her long asphalt driveway because I wanted to traverse the entire property, from stem to stern, fore and aft. Progressively we covered a lot of territory. While generally I'd ask her if going here or there were okay, sometimes I took the initiative to strike out on my own to check out new areas. One day as we were sauntering down the driveway, a neighborhood dog appeared from the woods bordering it. Naively it started up the drive. When I saw him, only one thing occurred to me: "Get off my property, you mangy cur. I'll teach you a lesson you won't quickly forget."

Without a second's notice, I sped after the dog—and I do mean "sped." Motivation transformed me into a Ferrari with a V12 engine that can get to 120 mph in seven seconds. My tail whirled like an airplane propeller, pushing me forward. Adrenaline was coursing through every muscle and somehow compensating for my lack of walking balance. I was like a well-oiled machine: perfect in design and in execution. He ran for all he was worth down the driveway, yelping in pure unadulterated fear. He had much to fear as he headed for the street into the orchard beyond. If I would have caught that trespasser, I would have given him what for ... if it hadn't been for my new human.

Unfortunately for me she had quickly recovered from her jaw-dropping shock and ran after me. She was faster than I had expected, grabbing me just before I began to cross the street. Given that vehicles drove at forty miles per hour on the rural lane, I was likely to have been made into chopped liver had I actually run out into it.

That aside, if she hadn't intervened, it would have been woe betide the stupid dog. I was going to engrave this incident in his memory. As it turned out, that wouldn't have been necessary. The dog apparently learned immediately never to tangle with me again. He never returned. I have to admit it took me awhile to realize what I had done. I had never known I could do that ... and for that matter, never did it again. But, then again, I didn't have to.

There's something about the behavior of dogs that makes me wonder if they are super-risk takers or just plain dumb. A classic example is dogs running up to a fence or wall and just leaping over it as if they knew for certain it was clear and safe on the other side. But in most cases they have no idea what's on the other side. I mean it could be a cliff, deep hole filled with water, a venomous snake, or piece of sharp glass or metal. Cats would never do that unless they were in fear for their lives and had to keep going. In general, they'd jump onto the fence or wall then quickly reconnoiter, checking to see what was on the other side before deciding if it were smart to jump down there.

Anyway, after my dog chase, there was no question. I was "*The* George." I was king of the hill. The grand poobah. The head honcho. The big kahuna. Stumps or not, I was one cat not to be messed around with. Oh, yeah, man, I was hot stuff!

§§§

CHAPTER 10

RUCKUS

My name is "Ruckus." When I was rescued—well, I wasn't exactly "rescued"—I was a runty, twelve-week-old -old male kitten with bat-like ears, a sloping skull, long-black fur, splayed legs, and sometime-frog-like ambulation. My mom had had feline panleukopenia, distemper, when she was pregnant with my siblings and me. As a result, I was born with an underdeveloped cerebellum, a condition known as "cerebellar hypoplasia" (CH). That rendered me partially blind with four stiff splayed limbs, constant tremors, jerky movements, and a lack of balance and coordination. My eyes were almost always wide-open which gave me a delightful look of wonderment that camouflaged my obvious defects. If one could get past my disabilities, I was adorable.

Fortunately my siblings had been unaffected by the disease. I have no idea how that worked. Mom had difficulty getting me to suckle, especially with my outstretched legs in constant motion. Like many other animals dealing with ill or disabled babies, she finally had to abandon me to help her other babies survive. That's when her two humans took over my feeding.

How I came to be adopted— or fostered—was somewhat surprising, I guess. The humans whose cat bore me brought me on a Sunday into an adoption clinic held by a no-kill, all-volunteer shelter at the local pet supplies' store. I was wrapped in a colorful beach towel covered in penguins. My humans got the adoption clinic manager's attention and said they didn't know what to do with me. They were afraid I'd get underfoot at home, have further CH-related health problems, or hurt myself since I didn't respond as other cats do to people, obstacles, and dangers.

They spread out the towel to demonstrate my problems with maneuvering. When placed on the towel, I lay on my side and energetically twisted and wriggled my kitten body to aid my legs as they tried to pull me along. My flailing limbs prevented me from moving in a straight line. I was more like a molecule in random motion. If I intended to go north, I would invariably end up east or west.

When my humans held me upright, I again attempted to achieve a forward movement. But instead of walking, I lunged. I almost hopped like a frog, but went back a half-step for every step in my desired direction. Released again, I immediately flopped over. I was down more than I was up. But, that didn't matter to me. I was eagerness personified. All bright-eyed and bushy tailed. I loved having an audience and all the attention that went with it. If I could sort of make eye contact, I signaled pick me up some more.

Lacking both balance and coordination made worse by my tremors, I couldn't move to where my food was. Some cats with moderate CH could eat and drink on their own despite their jerkiness but I was at the other end of the spectrum. And even when placed beside my food and water dishes on the floor, I couldn't raise my head and upper body to eat or drink on my own. When I was supported over the food, I would try to exercise control and do it on my own. But because of my constant movement, I'd often fall into my food and water, at risk of suffocating or drowning. As much as I wanted to, there was no way I could do it on my own. I had to be hand-fed.

Despite these "minor discrepancies," deviations from the norm, I was very soft and cuddly with a loud purr which began reverberating the moment anyone touched me. Pick me up? Yes, I loved being held. I was a total people-kitty and very tolerant of other animals, including other cats. When cradled on a lap, I was a mass of jumbled movements, except that my legs, unlike some cats with CH, were stiff and permanently jutting out from my body.

One of the volunteers at the adoption clinic that day was an individual who cared for disabled cats. She examined me closely,

116

tickling me. I made a grab for her nose but she probably couldn't tell because my front paw flung itself up and down nowhere near her face. I could tell she had a concern about the progressive likelihood of my condition. But with a large smile she adopted me. That proved what I knew to be absolutely true. Despite everything, I was truly adorable.

At her home she kept me in a very large cage, with all the essentials I needed. I was so tiny and dysfunctional I knew she was concerned for my safety. She took me out of the cage to pet, brush, and feed me. They could hear me purr across the street. Such heavenly delights were mine being touched and cuddled. Then her old, heavy-set male black cat, who looked as if he had barely survived the Gulf War and Afghanistan, took me under his wing. He was the only cat who came near me, except initially when the others inspected me out of curiosity. In spite of my Parkinsonian movements, he groomed me with his huge pink tongue, played with me, and showed me what every young kitten should know. He was so gentle and sweet.

I tried to follow him around but he walked straight like a lobster and I walked sidewise like a crab. However, in truth, most of the time my "walking" consisted of my lying on my side doing a spastic version of the sidestroke to move from point A to point B by way of point M. At least I was on carpeting which gave me a rough texture on which to work. My rescuer had secured a thick towel to the bottom of my cage so I could pull myself around.

After a week my level of physical inadequacy began to distress my feline mentor. He seemed to sense something was very wrong as I twitched and jerked even more, making it difficult for him to get near me. He was no longer comfortable being around me. I was not acting like any kitten he had encountered before. I was not picking up his lessons as he expected, even given all the latitude he had provided me. He began backing away, seeing me less often, finally ignoring me. He was never unkind just suddenly distant. I didn't understand what the problem was but was happy he had shown me such nurturance and loving care for the time he did. My rescuer picked up where the old male left off.

117

Even though I recognized I had a low-sided pan filled with litter in which to eliminate, I couldn't successfully scale the obstacle lying on my side to use it properly. Consequently, I always messed on myself and the towel on the cage floor. My rescuer discovered the problem quickly and was able to remedy it. While I was not crazy about being wet and messy, I didn't mind being bathed so frequently and towel dried. Nice warm towel on a chilled body. Being touched was always calming.

After putting in new floor towels several times a day, she soon removed them permanently. That left a slick metal floor which she covered with oilcloth, which likewise was slick. Even though she could clean it more easily, my movement within my cage became restricted. It wasn't a great tradeoff for either of us.

It was at this time that my rescuer took over teaching me. She leaned me against the living room wall and encouraged me to move. Always up for some fun, I tried hopping. I couldn't believe it. I actually sort of made a step or two before I fell over. She picked me up and I tried it again. I managed to get to three steps. My enthusiasm exploding, I gave it all I had. I was "walking." Well, hop-walking. It was a stupendous feeling of accomplishment. Every time she brought me out of my cage, which was frequently each day for cleaning me and the cage and feeding me, I increased my distance. Maybe I had a triathlon for the disabled in my future after all. My outlook was always sunny to begin with but I had never dreamed it could feel this good.

I tried using this wall-leaning technique to be more effective at eating and drinking in my cage. I waved my legs against the cage floor and flopped back and forth. When near the vertical bars, I tried to push myself closer to food and water which were within reach assuming I could get myself there. Even with splayed legs, if only I had been a little coordinated, it would have been easier.

But my maneuvering to attempt on this leaning behavior on my own was quickly forsaken. With my increasing body tremors and my ever-stiff limbs, there was no way I could conceivably raise myself on my own. I wanted to prove to myself I could reach my food and water on my own, that I didn't have to continue to be fed like a baby. But no matter how hard I tried, it was for naught. There was no way I could reach my food and water on my own even though they were close to the floor. This was quite frustrating.

I had no idea what was happening. My rescuer saw my efforts and held my body such that my face and mouth were in the proper position so she could lower me to eat and drink on my own. This lasted for only a day or two. My further decreasing lack of control of my limbs caused her to abandon this self-feeding effort. I was going to have to stay on the eye dropper.

As weeks passed, my rescuer was with me nearly all the time now. She sat on the floor beside the cage with her papers, laptop, and phone. It wasn't long before I started convulsing, slipping out of consciousness with grand mal episodes. She'd put her works aside, lift me out of my cage and cuddle me. She soothed me with her petting, soft words, and medications to ease my seizures. As my seizures quickly accelerated, however, the phenobarbital prescribed for them had less and less effect. I was unconscious, my body rigid, more often than I was conscious.

Leaving her work in her office, she now spent most of her time rocking me like a human baby. In between convulsions I looked at her and tried to pat her face. I tried my best to let her know how much I appreciated everything she had done for me. But she already knew. It was a reflection of the framed words on the living room wall, she told me about, that read: "Love is the absence of judgment," a quotation from the Dalai Lama XIV. She snuggled closer and smiled back at me. It was all-embracing. Despite my physiological functioning having finally fully regressed, I communicated to her that these six weeks with her had been a wonderful, fun, and unexpected gift for which I was supremely grateful.

§§§

CHAPTER 11

DOBBY

When a rescuer found me next to a dumpster, I was a four-month-old, tiny ball of gray fluff, ill and in pain. I only vaguely recall what had happened. I think I may actually have been *in* the open dumpster, trying to find my mother, and fell out. How I didn't break anything or damage something internally I'll never know. It's seems hard to believe now that I somehow used my innate twisting talent to fall on my feet, especially at that short distance. What I did know was that I was all alone. Hunger pangs constricted my gut like a python eager for a meal. I was so hungry that I had tried to eat anything I could find. Grasses enticed me. Of course, as I later discovered, they all came up with a vengeance.

Unknowingly, I had also sampled a weed called a foxtail. They looked like wheat seductively waving in the morning's breeze. Their golden seed heads stood upright with long antennae, seeking to beseech the gods for rain. Each short seed looked deceptively benign. In truth they were as sharp as X-Acto-blades and would stick permanently into anything that touched them. Fortunately this one didn't go down my gullet with the grass. But not much better, it stayed in my mouth, stabbing me. As I tried to extricate it, it penetrated the roof of my mouth. Burrowing as a dog creating a temporary burial vault for a bone, it dug its way through my hard palate into my right eye.

The resulting pressure and infection which affected both eyes was indescribably exquisite even in one so young. The seed caused my right eye to enlarge then bulge. If this had been in the 1950s, I would have been a shoe-in for some atomic horror flick—a kitty

Quasimodo without the hump, rampaging. Not surprisingly, it took little time for both eyes to fill with bacterial exudate. Multiple infections raged, further shoving my right eyeball out of its socket. By the time I was rescued, my ballooning right eye was nearly resting on my cheek.

Did I see a veterinarian? I don't know. But some human applied what I assumed was an antibiotic ointment to both eyes. Was it some leftover erythromycin a rescuer had? I wasn't sure at the time—I was glad someone was doing something—but it seemed a useless treatment for my nearly detached eyeball. Whoever it was continued to apply the ointment but it didn't help one bit. In fact, both eyes worsened significantly as did the pain as the ointment oozed into my right eye socket.

I hoped this person wasn't a professional. I would have expected a professional to have examined me, discovered the cause of my obvious problem, and determined the appropriate treatment regimen. No one did anything about the embedded foxtail seed. No one removed it. No one checked to see what bacteria were destroying my eyes. No one apparently knew what antibiotics to employ. No one knew what to do with my bulging eye or my left eye forced closed with nasty, burning goop.

When another rescuer saw me, she volunteered to take me. Finally the fates were with me. She had some medical background and knew the kind of help I needed ... and needed immediately. That time is still a little fuzzy since I was in and out of consciousness because of the infections. I couldn't see through my right eye and could barely detect light in my left when I risked trying to open it. This, however, didn't dampen my desire to reach out longingly for my mom or search for a little food as I rode the nauseatingly undulating asphalt to an emergency veterinary practice.

Like my two rescuers, the veterinarian treated me kindly and gently. While that didn't as yet stop the pain, it helped lessen my anxiety. She examined me carefully. Upon opening my mouth, she saw the embedded foxtail seed. Examination of my right eye told her that it was damaged beyond repair. She also looked at the eye pus under a microscope then gathered samples to be cultured in a petri dish in a laboratory. She had to know precisely what to prescribe for the infections. The use of the unknown "antibiotic" ointment that had been applied earlier had only prevented my being seen right away by a qualified person. I'm sure the human was trying to help but didn't know what to do that was appropriate. A professional who was ready and able to do what was medically necessary maybe could have saved my eyes, or at least one of them.

By now it was obvious there was no way to save my right eye. My new rescuer okayed the veterinarian removing it as well as digging out the resistant, embedded foxtail seed. So I lost one eye. That was a fait accompli. But could they save the other? Because the vet could see one specific bacterium under her microscope, she started me on an appropriate antibiotic, not erythromycin, as she awaited the results of the cultures to address other bacteria or viruses.

Talk about being out of luck. The results were not good. Among other infectious agents in my left eye, I had the most damaging and painful feline herpesvirus (FHV-1). Having created corneal ulcers, it had left noticeable scarring. Altogether, it took a series of antibiotics and antiviral eye drops to address each of the four infections. Afterward, I had to continue on l-lysine, an amino acid dietary supplement that had been found to inhibit herpes viral replication in the laboratory. However, there was no cure for the herpes virus. An outbreak could recur at any time. Ironically, I managed to keep the eye—an opening which revealed only white scar tissue—even though it was too damaged to allow any light or sight whatsoever. At least the pain and pressure were now a thing of the past.

After recovering from the trauma and infections, I found that time was actually on my side. Having been a baby when I lost my sight, I had had little experience seeing and using sight to navigate. I hadn't as yet come to depend on my eyesight to be a cat and do what cats do. Instead I had to develop, with the help of my new human, what's called a cognitive map in my brain. My companion knew that if I were to get around on my own in my new home, she would have to make sure that everything remained the same. She would not move any of the furniture or put any objects down in my path, at least until I developed my map. She wanted me to learn where everything was so I could become as comfortable and capable as possible moving from one room to the next. It was like painting brush strokes of color on a gray canvas.

For the most part she allowed me to roam unfettered but monitored my activities. Knowing I could startle easily when actions happened that I didn't expect, she always spoke before petting me. Her monitoring was also necessary so she could respond to my being panicked by a loud noise or rapid movements of other cats. If something startled me, I ran, like any sighted cat. But in my panic, I totally forgot my cognitive map and ran into furniture or walls. When I slammed into objects, it was primarily my pride more than my body that was bruised because of my whiskers. These sensitive touch receptors helped me gauge object distances and vibrations in the air even at full tilt.

One of my joys was encountering fresh catnip. From first sniff, I was entranced. I had had no idea such a psychedelic narcotic existed. When my companion presented leaves to me, I touched them with my nose and the tip of my tongue. Next I raised my head with my mouth partially open, rolled back my upper lip, wrinkled my nose, and inhaled deeply. I could feel a rush of intoxicating particles in the air. I didn't maintain that flehmen pose for long. When my brain said, "Go for it!" I immediately attacked the leaves with gusto.

My next challenge was to get to the second floor of the house. As yet I had no way to envision what lay ahead of me so I approached those steps with great trepidation. I didn't know what they were or what was at the end of a climb, if they actually ended. Would the floor fall away once I reached the top of them? Once I was up there, then what would I do? What was it they said about approaching a challenge? Right: No guts no glory. I couldn't let my fears and trepidations stop me. I could hear the other cats climb and make comments about me being stuck on the first floor. But not for long, I told myself. I knew I had to behave like the

Lewis and Clark of the blind cat world, venturing into the unknown, without a detailed map.

With nothing to fear ... but more humiliation ... I tried them. Climbing onto the first step was awkward. I couldn't face forward because the step was narrow and there was something—a small overhang of some sort—in front of me. If I were to stand on the step, I had to turn my body sideways. But sideways didn't help my forward motion. Padding around on the flat carpeted surface that had been in front of me, I discovered it was configured in a similar manner to what I was already sitting on. Okay. Reorienting my body to go forward, I pulled myself up on the next step. I can do this, I thought. Between each step I rested, feeling increasingly proud of myself, then went back to the task.

It took quite a while to ascend all fifteen steps. I had to make sure that my assumption about each succeeding step being like the last was correct. Amazingly, there *was* a floor up there where the stairs ended. I explored and explored. It was fascinating finding out what lurked behind the four doors off a hallway. But once I finished the "journey of the corps of discovery" à la Ken Burns, I was faced with an even more daunting task: climbing back down. This took lots longer because I had to lean over into the void, pawing the air, patting with a front paw to see where the next step down was. The possibility of falling into space was evident and did not make me happy.

Initially, I discovered that I could twist my body to the side, as I had on the first step going up, and hunker down so I could use the length of the stair step to help me reach the next one below. But whenever another cat or my human walked up or down the stairs, I had to start all over again in my mind. Descent was tough but I ultimately did manage all fifteen stairs. To do so I had to keep that number foremost in my mind so I didn't over- or under-shoot the bottom.

Pretending I was doing it for exercise, I practiced until I had a good mental picture of what and where. I am pleased to share that soon I was nonchalantly ascending and descending the stairs. And I was facing forward, mind you, irrespective of who was walking on them or stretched out on them. This garnered lots of well-deserved praise from my human.

My next accomplishment was locating the island in the kitchen and leaping onto it. Like most cats, or so I've heard, I like heights. I also like being closer to my human when she talks to me. Closer also makes it easier for her to pet me. My leaping really surprised my human who worried I might come too close to the edge, lose my balance, and fall off. O, human, of little faith. As it turned out, the only time that happened was when a newspaper lay open on the island, draped slightly over the side. I stepped on it where I expected the island to be... and down I went. Again, I was bruised but not hurt enough to complain about or go to the vet.

Although my cognitive map was flawless, as far as it went, it didn't take into account that my human might have an island drawer open just as I attempted one of my Olympic leaps. Thump! I collided with the bottom of the utensils drawer with my head. Quickly my human was on her knees checking me out, gently petting my sore cranium, and speaking calmingly to me. Once was enough. She never again used that drawer whenever I was around. Not to be dissuaded, I regained my confidence and continued to jump upon that side of the island. You can still do what you want once you've properly trained your human to put your needs first. Their guilt helps speed the process.

After I had mastered the stairs, I put whipped cream and a cherry on top of my climbing accomplishment. I began running up the stairs. Soon thereafter, I began running down the stairs. I was GOOD—"hot damn!" From then on, I checked out all the furniture, any ladders that were set up, shelves, and the television cabinet. I climbed and leaped up and down with abandon. My confidence was getting bigger and stronger as if I were on emotional steroids. I could locate my human and other cats with ease.

But my *pièce de résistance* was when a mouse was foolish enough to invade my domicile. Contrary to the other cats' renditions of this incident, *I* was the one who heard its scampering first. *I* was the one who followed it as it ran under the stove, wove its way around chair legs and slipped under the dining room hutch. As the other cats gathered around, heads low, sniffing, *I* was the one to run after it when it broke loose. And— trumpets please—*I* was the one—*the* one—who grabbed that furry little trespasser by the back of its neck, sat down in front of the semi-circle of bereft cats, and growled for them to keep away from *my* prize. Gotcha, sucka!

Sadly, my human arrived and unceremoniously removed the still-live mouse from my "jaws of death" and released it outside. You know how humans are! That meant I wasn't going to get to gnaw on any mouse guts—not that that was of any particular interest to me. I did want to gloat for a while longer however. But, no, she couldn't let me continue to show off. Ah, well. Irrespective, I had demonstrated to all who was *the* mouser *par excellence*. And I did it better than they did and without my sight.

And, just to keep my reputation alive, whenever a mouse had managed to skitter in again, I was there, clinching my new prize, ever triumphant. Even without this one sense, I was in every respect a fully-functioning Super Cat, the understandable envy of all. And, to my fans, of whom there are many, I thank you for your acclaim and support.

§§§

CHAPTER 12

PAULA

There is no question that I am a striking orange tabby, short-haired domestic cat with dark swirling rust markings on a long, slim body, Baltic amber eyes lightly outlined in black, and a broad nose. The fur on my nose consists of curved tufts of hair which diagonally cross to the bridge, making me look as if I might have had some abstract body art surgery. Beneath my luxurious white whiskers and on the tip of my chin are small patches of white, offsetting the rest of my dramatic coloring. My nostrils and lips are bright pink and spotted with black. "Deliciously exotic like a rare tropical flower" is how I'd describe my look.

And I'm female. You can call me "Paula." I've been told that female orange tabbies are rare, which would seem appropriate in my case. But, alas, that's just not so. We're just not as common as the males. And who wants to be "common" anyway. To complete the picture I have to add that I don't meow per se. I'm graced with a lower-pitched voice which sounds a Lauren Bacall chirp. It suits me.

While it felt as if I had been a long-time resident of a companion animal and medical assistance group, I had been there only several months, brought in as a ten-month-old adolescent. Even though I was friendly and enjoyed a good scratch, I wasn't all that interested in being held or sitting on a human's lap. So when potential adopters came into the cattery to meet us potential adoptees, some thought me persnickety or "stuck on myself." I thought I was simply being more discerning, expressing my preferences, choosing what I wanted to do. But this behavior seemed to discourage a lot of humans who expected something more ... or different.

If they wanted me to beg for attention and do just about anything to acquire it, they could forget it. Sorry. I wasn't going to act like a dog, doing whatever a human wanted in order to be liked. Getting attention is great but I have to be true to myself above all else. I think of myself as an independent cat ... a principled feline.

That was pretty much how I felt until a volunteer came in several times a week for an hour each to help socialize those of us who had been on our own for a long time and not with humans. She played with us, talked to us, and generally listened. I took a fancy to her. When she sat on a sofa in one of the cattery rooms, I made a point of rubbing against her leg then jumping onto her lap. When I'm in the mood to snuggle, I'm the best snuggler.

I nuzzled her, pressing my head against her chest. Then I raised my honey-tinted eyes to look up at her and flashed a come-hither kitty smile. I knew it would melt both her heart and brain then and there. It was particularly important that I "melt her brain," her resolve, because I knew she already had a number of rescue cats and was less likely to adopt another of us any time soon.

However, I don't want you to think I was pretending. I wasn't. There was something so familiar about her. Something I sensed. It was as if she had been my identical twin in another incarnation. And I don't know if I even believe in reincarnation. To me dead is dead. But, with her I felt a genuine, deep connection. I wanted to touch her and be touched by her and be with her forever.

I know she felt it too because it wasn't long before she adopted me to join her already large brood. Despite all the other felines desiring her attention, I always felt the attention I received was special. It wasn't necessarily more than the others received, but it had a more personal and spiritual meaning. To put it telepathically, she could read my mind and I hers. I felt we were not only emotionally- but also physically linked. I became *her* soul cat—and she my *soul* human companion.

Whatever she wanted I provided if I could. This included allowing her to pick me up, be placed in her lap or around her shoulders, be brushed and stroked. I also enthusiastically jumped onto her lap. We touched and cuddled a lot. While I still needed time to myself, I was with her nearly every moment she was nearby. That did not include riding in the car, however, except when we traveled to the vet. I hated going anywhere in the car. The motion and car smell always resulted in nausea and vomiting which ruined my entire day.

After eleven years of excellent health, watching movies together, like the 1956 "Invasion of the Body Snatchers," snuggling under a quilt on the sofa on a snowy evening, and enjoying our companionship, I started having intestinal problems. It started with a little diarrhea but increased over time. As it became chronic, I also experienced frequent, abdominal pain, bloating, gas, vomiting, nausea, and passage of small amounts of feces and mucus. I was uncomfortable, odiferous, and didn't like being around myself.

Initially the vet suggested that the cause might be dietary intolerances, allergies, dietary fiber deficiency, emotional mental distress, or changes in my colon. When she tested for parasites, bacteria, and lower abdominal masses, she found nothing to account for it except my lower intestine looked a little inflamed on x-ray, suggesting Irritable Bowel Disorder. She recommended a change to a hypo-allergenic food; FortiFlora, a probiotic to increase good bacteria in my gut; sub-cutaneous fluids to keep me hydrated since I lost so much body water with the diarrhea; and Depo-Medrol, a steroid to ease the inflammation.

I can't say that all the recommendations were effective. The prescription food had a disgusting flavor and mush-like texture. I don't know how cats can get it down without immediately barfing it back up. And that's expensive stuff. The animal food companies must be making a fortune on it because all vets prescribe it in some form. I didn't bother after the first lick. As if that weren't bad enough, the FortiFlora made it an inedible mess that I tried to cover. It belonged in my litter pan. I continued the steroid, an injection every six weeks. That lasted for about a year because it seemed to be the only treatment that might be helping. But despite my scheduled six-week check-ups at the vet, I was slowly losing weight. My appetite was still intact so this was not a good sign.

On its heels other things began to change. I started losing my appetite. Then, horror of horrors, I started losing control of my bowels. Because I was feeling pressure to eliminate anywhere and everywhere, I found myself continually embarrassed. I wanted to hide in shame. Soon thereafter, things became much worse. I started to drip and leave a small puddle wherever I walked or sat. For a super-fastidious cat, this was anathema. When my human noticed, she didn't say anything to me for which I was grateful. I was already completely humiliated. She just cleaned up the mess on the sofa, on the floor, or on her lap, and gave me mini-bath as well. While I needed it, I didn't need to be reminded why. But soon the constant fecal drizzle was replaced by a viscous bloody mucus and pus which signaled seriously infected tissue.

The moment my human spotted this, I was back at the vet—by now the clinic had virtually become my home away from home—where upon I was x-rayed again. The lower intestine wall had become much thicker demonstrating that the inflammation was much worse. The Depo-Medrol wasn't helping enough—maybe it never did or maybe it did initially but apparently was no longer effective. Who knew?

My physical appearance had altered so slowly that neither my human nor vet noticed how cadaverous I had become. It was like a frog placed in a pot of water which is heated so slowly the frog never notices the change until the heat kills it. I know that's an unconscionable human experiment but it's the best analogy I can conjure up for how everyone missed the change. I was sent on an emergency referral to a specialist for an ultrasound.

With my abdomen shaved, I was then anesthetized. My innards were examined from without with sound waves. Pictures were taken followed by fine needle biopsies. The images revealed a suspicious-looking, highly thickened wall of my lower intestine. The cells of which spelled out a message in flickering lights two feet high: "small-cell gastrointestinal lymphoma." The prognosis? Without immediate intervention I was not long for this world. The way I felt it was perhaps a good thing.

My human and I met with their world-renown veterinary oncologist, Dr. Barbara Kitchell, who thoroughly examined me and went through my entire history. She looked at all my diagnostic results and treatments and suggested I go on a regimen of chlorambucil, prednisolone, Vitamin B-12 injections, and sub-cutaneous fluids.

Chlorambucil, brand name Leukeran, is chemotherapy which has achieved much success with cats with cancer in research programs. The prednisolone, which had to be specially compounded, is a steroid that is better suited to handling this kind of inflammation than the Depo-Medrol or prednisone. Because my diarrhea had inhibited absorption of Vitamin B-12 in my gut, I had a deficiency. B-12 is necessary for red blood cell health and production, appetite, energy, and keeping my nerves in tip top working order. The sub-cutaneous fluids were to hydrate me by replacing all I was losing through the diarrhea and keep all parts of my body functioning properly. And last but not least were the antibiotics for the intestinal abscesses.

I started on the vile 2 mg. cancer pill twice a week. Because it is powerful stuff, it required my human to handle it wearing latex gloves. The prednisolone was a liquid that I had to endure orally on a daily basis along with the liquid antibiotics. Incredibly, within one week, I was eating again ... and enjoying eating. Within two weeks, I was actually feeling almost perky. Life looked more hopeful. I felt like cuddling again ... and could now do so without leaving an unpleasant trace after I left.

I had learned from my human that French psychologist Émil Coué grounded his psychotherapy in self-improvement which he based on optimistic autosuggestion: "Every day in every way I'm getting better and better." It seemed to me to be worth a try. Humans with cancer are often encouraged to think positively and even imagine a white bear gobbling up their cancer cells. I kept telling myself I was feeling better and better ...and ... I did feel better and better. The polar bear image was harder for me to do. I didn't relate to polar bears though I was sure I eventually could.

I tried using a white dog. Alas, knowing what dogs will eat, that didn't work for me. It didn't really matter that the positive change was mostly due to the medications taking effect. But I know my positive attitude helped, as did my human's. Altogether, the change was astonishing.

I saw the oncologist once a month and kept improving so we didn't change my daily regimen. Months went by. I expressed an interest in checking out my human's gardens, something I had never done before. Earlier on I had become a full-time house cat and had no desire to revert to the wild-and-free life before my rescue. However, I was suddenly like a cat reincarnated, my curiosity soaring. I wanted to explore. I wanted to experience all I could with my human.

We sat on her deck in late afternoon and watched as the glorious orange globe floated toward the horizon in the west, painting the sky with pastel striations of pink, apricot, tangerine, lavender, and platinum, theatrically backlighting clouds. Then something gently landed on my head, between my ears. I brushed it off with my right front paw. It landed on my nose, tickling like mad. It was large, yellow with a delicate black border on its wings. It was a swallowtail butterfly. I looked at it cross-eyed until I thought I would sneeze. Suddenly it fluttered away, dipping its wings as if to acknowledge me. My human was laughing softly, but not at me. She too was amazed by the happening and the marvels that Nature holds for us if we're open to them. Having her there with me made it all ten times better. I got to enjoy her enjoyment as well. Life was wonderful, something to be cherished even more.

My gut continued to improve. I had finished the antibiotics ages ago. Hurrah! And there had been no recurrence of pus, mucus, or dripping. Tending to my toilette by myself was once again possible. I was looking like the Paula of old: gorgeous, sophisticated, yet sassy. I packed away the chow although I didn't gain more than a pound or two. I wasn't concerned about this because being so stylishly sleek I'd never weighed much. I naturally looked like a runway model, without the need of heavy smoking or bulimia.

About twelve months into my treatment my oncologist noticed that there were dark spots forming in the iris of my left eye. She had her ophthalmologist examine my exterior iris and the interior of my eye under magnification using a slit-lamp biomicroscope. While brown spots in the iris, referred to as hyperpigmentation or melanosis, are common, she was concerned about this happening in a cat with cancer. The pigment could represent a mole or tumor of the iris. That could be either benign or malignant. The exterior of the eye looked perfectly normal. Good because I felt fine. However, my human needed to monitor my left eye for any increase in the amount of pigment. We were to return in two months or sooner if necessary.

My relationship with my human was most satisfying, except for the administration of the chemo, prednisolone, B-12, and sub-Q fluids, of course. You really get tired of having the skin on your upper back poked with a large-gauge needle and your body flooded with one hundred milliliters of fluid twice a week. I was of a mind to stop her doing it. But the better I felt the more tolerant I became.

Over the next three and a half months the discoloration in my left eye increased. It was looking more like malignant melanoma than benign melanosis. The concern was that if it were melanoma, at some point melanoma cells might break off the tumor. They would then be free to float in the aqueous fluid of my eye and slip into my blood stream to circulate throughout my body. Because melanoma spreads rapidly the question arose: what to do about my left eye? The eye could be removed but that meant that whatever time I had left on chemo would be spent adjusting to seeing with only one eye.

That didn't make me happy and I told my human so. Likewise, she felt it would be cruel to add to my stress if I didn't have years ahead of me. She asked the ophthalmologist about the possibility of doing a fine needle aspiration biopsy of my eye to be sure it was cancer. The eye specialist said that though this procedure was done, she didn't recommend it. There was no way to be sure of capturing enough cells for testing, to be sure it was malignant. Furthermore, she didn't want to risk loosening melanoma cells, which were still intact, which could then begin to circulate.

At four months of increased discoloration my left eye began to ulcerate in two locations. The pain was beyond description. The scourge of cats, the feline herpesvirus-1 (FHV-1) had insinuated itself and would remain an infectious threat. I was given eye medications for the virus, an accompanying bacterial infection, and the pain. Ironically, in the mean time I was approaching the longest time any cat had survived on chlorambucil in research. My oncologist with whom I had developed a warm rapport regretfully told my human that there was nothing else to try for my lower intestine when this chemo began to lose its ability to keep the lymphoma in check.

As I entered the fifth month of my eye problem, the initial ulcerations had healed. I continued the anti-viral and pain drops. My left eye felt better but my sight was impaired by the scarring. But at least I still had sight in it. Now, however, I had begun losing weight again. Talk about tradeoffs. The ulcers had cleared but my handsome coat was beginning to look as scruffy as it once again hung on my rapidly-developing skeletal body. It was as if I had had a bath and no one brushed my coat as I dried.

I was becoming more fatigued by the day and intestinal discomfort was not so slowly returning. In order to keep me with her so she could keep an eye on me, my human created a sling from an old gray sweat shirt which she tied around her neck and over her shoulder and pinned together. Like conjoint twins we walked around the house and garden. I was at her side as she worked in her office.

Communicating frequently, my human and I weighed what was going on versus what I wanted. I wanted to stay with her as long as possible. But, I also wanted to slip away as soon as necessary. Caught on the horns of this dilemma, I watched as my ribs, spine, and hipbones protruded sharply. I saw objects and activities that had intrigued and stimulated me before slip through the cracks of my interest, including catnip which my human grew for her cats. The only exception was my human's touch. I still lived for that connection. It mitigated the discomfort somewhat. Yet I had to decide. It was obvious to me the time had come. Our last hug where she and I became one will always stay with me in the ether waves.

I had been living on borrowed time. Because of the chemotherapy I had been granted a one-year and nearly five-month reprieve, something I would never have had without it. It was truly a miracle. I was an evangelist for it and my oncologist. Given that extraordinary opportunity, I had made the most of it every day, even when the encroaching melanoma of my iris appeared.

My human and I would never grow old together, I reluctantly accepted that. But, then again, no one had ever been luckier than I that we had found each other. In the end she was the one who liberated me from fear, need, and pain. We were, and always would be, *one*. I rejoiced in that as she bade me farewell.

§ § §

CHAPTER 13

TONY

I won't go much into my early life except to say I had been on my own on the streets a while—I was about four-years-old—before the accident happened. I was crossing the street when BAM! A speeding car clipped my rear end, sending me flying onto the concrete sidewalk. I have no knowledge of how long I lay there before some human—the driver of the vehicle or some Good Samaritan who wandered by—took me to an animal shelter. A shelter? Why not a veterinary clinic? Initially the shock obscured the pain that was soon to appear and overwhelm me.

I barely recall my transportation to the city shelter. I knew I was being moved repeatedly. Once admitted, I was placed in a cage on a cold concrete floor. I lay there, barely able to move. As I was beginning to make sense of it all, I found that my front legs worked but my back legs trailed out behind me, seal-like, but as a dead weight. The pain in my lower back and legs was excruciating. When I tried to drag myself around, I thought I would pass out from it.

Time crept by as I waited patiently for someone to examine, x-ray, and help me—at the very least with the pain. I needed help big time. But no one came. I waited and waited. The only human I saw was a worker at the shelter who when he wasn't sweeping out cages brought me a small bowl of dry food and water. I could be half-dead or dying—and felt that way—for all anyone seemed to care. I continued to lie there all alone, in agony.

As I took stock of my anatomy and physical state, I experienced a revelation. There was no way I could use the litter pan. While I might be able to slide my body over to it, pain aside, there was no way I could hike myself up, over the lip, and into it. And furthermore, not that it mattered that much in these particular circumstances, I had no longer had any control over my bladder. As a result, my previous long, luxurious caramel-apple-colored fur, especially on my rear end and tail, were soon to be always wet and covered in feces. I waited and waited and waited for someone to clean me but no one did. Mixed with my fur, my waste was creating adobe-like slurry on my tail and back legs which would no doubt harden into a layered plaster cast.

Potential adopters came by to look at cats. They were entranced by my big amber eyes set in a broad and sweet leonine face. They were impressed by my glorious lion's mane. But the moment they glanced into my cage and observed that I couldn't stand and was covered in a disgusting, coffee-grounds-looking mess, they hurried on. I could feel the skin on my back legs and tail burning from the trapped acidic urine and feces. I could tell from the way the visitors and shelter workers regarded me, holding their noses, that I was seen as worthless—not worth bothering with—and, therefore, not long for this world.

I wasn't worthless. What did I have to do to show them that? But I knew I couldn't do it all by myself. Why didn't someone care? Someone needed to care. About my situation I was torn. I wanted to die if I had to live there as I was. I was a prisoner in my own body and no one seemed to give a damn one way or the other. My back and leg pain and overall discomfort increased by the day as did my sense of hopelessness. Maybe I could learn to walk again if only someone mitigated the pain and chipped away at my lower-body cast.

At the same time a wee small voice within me uttered the hope that a kitty miracle could happen: that I could be invited by some caring person to live with them. I knew the probabilities of that were slim to none, but I still hoped it down in the inner recesses of my big cat heart. Unfairness may be a human concept but I knew, if only I were given the chance, I could make things better for myself and a human companion. Someone, please, just give me a chance.

Not to get all religious about it—cats don't hold religious beliefs—but apparently miracles *can* and sometimes actually *do* happen! Totally out of the blue one morning a rescuer came by to see if there were any cats their no-kill group might be able to place for adoption. City shelters didn't seem to do much, from my perspective, to try to get cats ... or dogs for that matter ... adopted.

Even in the short time I was imprisoned there, I had seen too many human pet companions come looking for their pets after they'd already called the pound to alert them and ask about their pet. These were all-too-familiar stories of concerned companions who had done everything conceivable to locate their microchipped dog or cat only to discover their beloved pet had been at the shelter when they'd called and had been euthanized almost immediately irrespective of the shelter having been notified. This was the pounds' dirty little secret, only it wasn't so little or secret.

In my case, as the rescuer walked by my cage, I looked up at her with my soft eyes, meowed, and told her I needed assistance badly and now: ASAP! To make the point I raised my right front paw and patted the wire cage door forlornly. When she saw my desperate condition, she quickly called the president of her local shelter for homeless companion animals. The non-profit's president raced over to take me under her wing. I had never seen the blood vessels in a human's temples stand out as hers did. I had never seen such an apoplectically-red face when she examined my pitiful condition. Grumbling to herself in a language that cats do not use, even when yowling to announce "love for sale," she roused the shelter supervisor and made a point of giving him a razor-sharp tongue lashing. Not mincing words, she stated there was no excuse possible for what had *not* been done for me. It was neglect and abuse and perhaps possible criminality. The newspapers and local TV news crews should hear about it: they would truly love it. From the way the supervisor reacted, he was clearly embarrassed and defensive.

His excuses about not getting the best workers or not having enough funding fell on deaf ears. In all her years of rescuing homeless companion animals, providing medical assistance to them, and trying to work with the system to improve it, she had heard this standard operating procedure, bureaucratic rationalization doo-doo before. The point was they were not doing their job responsibly. I had been neglected and abused. She signed the adoption papers and gingerly carried me out to her SUV where she placed in the back on a blanket. As we left, the supervisor who was standing in the door wiped the sweat from his curled his upper lip and gave her the finger. For me it was "free at last, free at last." The sun seemed brighter than I had ever recalled.

She immediately conveyed me to a veterinarian. The pain of being moved into and out of the car then examined from head to foot and x-rayed was bad. But her concern and the vet's care seemed to ameliorate it to a small degree. Afterward, the vet arrived at a diagnosis. From being hit by the car, I had sustained spinal nerve damage resulting in partial paralysis of my rear legs and incontinence. However, the vet added that with specific physical therapy I might be able to regain some ambulatory ability—well, you know, sort of "walk." My hip and leg bones apparently still had the potential to hold me up to a degree. My muscles and nerves required a workout regimen. But if I ever learned to walk again, my rear end would likely meander sideways. Moreover, I'd probably drag my right leg a little.

Removing the sheets of solidified feces from my long coat and previously luxurious tail took a lot of effort and even more time. Then the rescue volunteers had to shave me. I would not put this procedure in the "comfortable" column. Each little hair pull caused me to wince. Some hair was so encased in feces right on down to my skin that the electric razor occasionally nicked my tender, often raw, burning skin. At least they didn't have to cut my still magnificent, shaggy mane. They bathed me and put ointment on all the inflamed areas which made me look as if I'd rolled in Vasoline. Oooh. Icky sticky. They placed me loosely in a large towel.

After they had done all the required blood tests and gotten their results, they finally gave me a sub-cutaneous injection of slow-release buprenorphine between my shoulder blades to ease my pain. It took between fifteen and thirty minutes to fully take effect but when it did, I almost felt alive again. Amazing what a little morphine-like opioid can do. Whaa-hoo!

I couldn't believe how incredibly lucky I had been to have a human really see and hear me, much less care about what they had seen and heard. From what I had seen daily, so many—in fact, maybe even most—weren't so lucky. The shelter humans and politicians said they had no money, no choice. What cat crap nonsense. They had the money and choice when they wanted to build a sports stadium or achieve some project dear to their hearts. The truth was our lives simply didn't matter, or matter enough, despite all the political lip-service paid to saving homeless cats and dogs.

That day I became a full-fledged member of a cat residence for homeless cats. Besides the three squares a day, I received lots of attention from my president human and her cattery volunteers. They made me their focus and employed various methods to get me to exercise, to strengthen my rear end, and hopefully improve my chances of walking. We weren't enclosed in cages so I could walk around all I wanted, which was exactly what I needed. I also had weekly appointments with a vet who was an animal acupuncturist. I don't think it's my imagination that the needles actually helped somewhat. I was beginning to stand and create some semblance of waddling along. I daydreamed I could be King of the Beasts once again.

One of the volunteers who came twice a week to help socialize us cats for adoption decided she wanted to adopt me. Every time she came in, I felt lighter. I'd hobble-drag-trot over to her for petting and scratching under my chin. I'd stare seductively at her with my big, Dijon-mustard-colored eyes, telling her how much I liked her and would gladly live with her. And with every surge of excitement, my bladder let go. Oops!

She was always encouraging me to go just a little farther than I thought I could. One of the things she encouraged was for me to try to get on her lap. She sat on a low sofa in one of the cattery rooms, called me by name, clapped her hands, and gave me a big smile. How could I not respond positively to that?

Even though I tried valiantly to get on her lap, I never quite managed to do it. The strength and coordination weren't there. I really wanted to accomplish that ... for both of us. I knew that if I kept trying, I would someday accomplish it. There was no way I'd stop trying, especially for her.

Leaky bladder and all, she chose *me* from all the other cats at the cattery, most of whom had no physical problems, to go to her home and live with her forever. "Deliriously happy" doesn't quite cover it.

Once in her home, I had so many places on the first floor to roam freely that I was always discovering something new. While her other cats looked askance at me when I arrived, they more or less accepted me over time. At least they didn't try to push me around. I felt I had passed through the pearly gates to kitty heaven ... except for the stairs.

Ah, yes, like another kitty before me, I met the infamous stairs to the second floor with chagrin. I wanted to explore the second floor where many of my compatriots rested during the day, looking over the top stair at those of us below. Would I ever be able to ascend much less descend them? I'd have a lot of work to do before that might even be a remote possibility.

My new companion was all about building and strengthening my lower back and legs. She likewise wanted me to be able to do more of what the other cats could and did do. Initially she concentrated on helping me remain upright. To do this she created what I thought was the cat equivalent of Tony Horton's P90X "muscle confusion" series for humans for me. Okay, so I couldn't really tell the difference between one TV exercise promotional gimmick and another. It could have been Pilates for all I knew. But it definitely wasn't Chuck Norris and the Total Gym or Richard Simmons' "Sweatin' to the Oldies."

One thing she did was flash a laser light on the wall or move it quickly along the floor. That was great because the red dot seemed alive. Other times she waved some reflective Mylar strips on the end of a long stick at me to encourage me to follow it with the hopes of ripping it to sparkly shreds. Each time she used the laser or Mylar, she added some other movements on which to focus, like reversing or going in circles or at angles, or raising it above my head so I'd try to stand on my back legs. It wasn't a chore; I actually enjoyed it and the treats and praise that went with it. However, I tired easily. Doing my workouts on a brick floor was lots easier than doing them on slick linoleum of the cattery.

She talked a lot to me as we went round the room and pieces of furniture at varying speeds. Her objective was to get me to walk and walk and walk. She even turned on her treadmill to a very slow speed and placed me on it, dropping treats ahead of me. She stood next to me as a safety measure as I walked on the flat and level. Then over time, I walked up inclines and down again. I heard her say she wished I could do this treadmill in water. But with my gorgeous long fur I wasn't interested in being soggy all the time.

To strengthen my abdominal muscles to better support my back she also put me on my side (or back when possible) and tickled my tummy. With each tickle my front and back legs tried to meet in the middle. At least there were no deep knee bends. As the vet predicted, there was still a lot of the expected side-slippage of my caboose as I chugged along. But I was moving along and getting better every time I did it. I was like the Little Engine That Could: "I think I can, I think I can."

Weeks and months went by. I could feel myself getting stronger and able to stay stably upright for much longer. I was wobbling less but still dragging my right leg a little. With all that preparation I was finally able to—dare I say it—climb onto her lap! Talk about a feeling of success! She made such a big deal out of it. I was so proud and pleased.

Using the cat pan had been a struggle at first but I was now becoming quite adept, even athletic, about getting in and out without stepping on the rim and dumping the litter all over the bricks. And, miracle of miracles, I was holding my urine better. That may not seem like much to most people, but to drippy ol' me it was a "BHAG," a *big hairy audacious goal* I had accomplished.

As the first year finished, the only time I urinated on the floor now was when I was startled by a loud noise or other cats running around me. My new companion showed understanding about my only-occasional accidents and praised me every time I used the litter pan to urinate. I had come a long way from the partially paralyzed cat lying in a jail cell. And I knew I could do so much more.

Every time I walked by the stairs, I sighed to myself, knowing there were wonderful discoveries up in that stratosphere but I was inadequate to ever reach them. My new companion saw me and asked, "Do you want to go upstairs?" I affirmed that with lifting my whiskers as I stared at the stairs—absolutely yes. "Okay," she replied. "Come over here."

She was standing by the stairs, clapping her hands with enthusiasm. I could never ignore such enthusiasm. I walked over. She placed my front paws on the carpeted first step. Sitting on the next step up to my right, she patted the stair on which she sat, "You can do it!" I struggled. I stepped on the first step. She praised me, moved up to the next one, and repeated the process. That day I had climbed three whole steps. Of course, getting back down took more than a little finagling but I did that too, with tremendous anxiety, until I reached the floor. It was exhausting. But the floor never looked so sweet: solid ground. Then I displayed my lion grin and shook my mane. What an accomplishment! Thanks, my mom-like human.

Every day thereafter I stood by the stairs to work on my mountain climbing, without a safety rope, harness, or pitons. I felt pretty klutzy at first but soon gained my balance and coordination on them. Practice, practice, practice. It took a week of strenuous activity with my human cheering me on. But when I reached the summit, I knew I had finally made it. I did it! I did it! I wanted to do a dance and shout, Look at me! Look at me! I'm the one! But the other cats didn't appear that interested aside from curiosity. Well, anyway, bully for me.

But then, of course, I had to make my way back down. One of my new compatriots was a blind cat who had already mastered the upstairs-downstairs procedure. But her trying to explain how to do it unsighted to someone sighted simply didn't work well. After a day of instruction, she apologetically begged off. I looked into the abyss, wondering if I really, really, really had to. Being upstairs at night had its benefits. If I could climb the stairs, I could climb onto my companion's low platform bed. But I didn't want to be an upstairs captive, away from all the downstairs daytime activity, brushing, petting, and treats. That meant I had to get working on my descension skills.

Whenever I leaned over the top step, it felt as if gravity were grabbing hold of me, threatening to throw me into the air and down the stairs. My heart thundered in my chest. Is this what fear of heights feels like? I positioned my front paws on the second to the top step, lined up my rear haunches, and let go. Down I plunged. I couldn't stop. I felt as if I were hurtling through space, barely touching the stairs I flew over. The bottom was fast approaching. What now? Amazingly as I hit the bottom, I was still on my feet. What the__? How in the world did I ever manage to do that? I was totally astounded by what I had done it. But ... but ... I had done it. Yes, I had!

Before long my cautious ascending and descending were old hat. I was one of the Rough Riders, charging up San Juan Hill with Teddy Roosevelt despite my draggy back leg. And getting back down now? Piece of cake. I ran down them under control too. No spills whatsoever. My new companion was delighted at *my* being so pleased with my achievement. I still may have walked a little funny but I was one of the Cat Pack, one cool cat.

But I should win the Oscar for my final trick. Wait a minute. Does the Academy of Motion Picture Arts and Sciences *still* give out awards for brilliant, talented animal actors? Anyway, there was an opening up four feet in the wall near the stairs which overlooked the living room. The other cats would often sit there one by one and survey their domain. Why not me? I asked. After days of practice revving up my engine and giving myself a good head start, I ran toward the wall using my back legs muscles to launch me. I leaped for all I was worth. Incredibly I landed in the opening! Even more amazing: I didn't go through.

I balanced there, as regal as regal could be. This was my kingdom too. I was the MGM lion—*Ars gratia artis*. Even better, when I jumped down, I made a perfect three-point landing (or four-point if you want to be anatomically correct). Unbelievably, my companion somehow caught my act. If only she had had a camera handy to memorialize this moment. This was the *crème de la crème*.

After that I didn't need to prove anything more to myself. I had my gorgeous fur once more. I was loved. I had amiable feline companions in a comfortable environment. And—best of all—I didn't have to wear kitty Depends! What more could the King of the Jungle ask for?

§ § §

ABOUT THE AUTHOR

Signe A. Dayhoff, PhD, is a social psychologist from Boston University with post-graduate training in counseling, emotional intelligence, and positive psychology. For over 30 years she has been a cognitive-behaviorist, coach, and author, specializing in increasing confidence and interpersonal communication skills and alleviating social anxiety. An applied feline behaviorist and cat rescue volunteer, she is kitty-mom to 20-plus senior and disabled cats. She consults on improving human-cat communication and relationships.

She has taught psychology at Boston University, University of Massachusetts, and Framingham State College and has done research at Massachusetts Institute of Technology, Fairview State Hospital (aka, Fairview Developmental Center), and Scripps Clinic and Research Foundation.

She is author of seventeen books: *Attracting and Dating the Wrong Men: Tips and Insights to Free Yourself; What Faust the Dancing Cat Taught Me; Growing Up "Unacceptable"—How Katharine Hepburn Rescued Me; How Insiders Get Jobs: 6-Mini-Course Series; Scared of Your Boss? Smash Through Your Fear Now; Promote Myself? I'd Rather Eat Worms!; How to Speak Without Fear Small Talk Course;* 2nd Ed. of *Diagonally-Parked in a Parallel Universe: Working Through Social Anxiety); Create Your Own Career Opportunities; Get The Job You Want;* and *Decision Making For Managers.* And she contributed to David Riklan's *101 Great Ways to Improve Your Life (Vol. 2)* and Steven J. Bennett's *Executive Chess: Creative Problem Solving By 45 of America's Top Business Leaders and Thinkers.*

§ § §

RESOURCES

Are you looking for tested, proven help with
- Social anxiety or social effectiveness?
- Confidence?
- Public speaking or small talk?
- Bosses or authority figures?
- Effective job hunting?
- Unacceptability and bullying?
- Dating the "wrong men"?
- Promoting or presenting yourself?
- Enjoying the pet-human bond
via the wild adventures of a dancing cat named Faust?

BOOKS (Kindle and Print):
Go to http://tinyurl.com/q4a3f3t
What Faust the Dancing Cat Taught Me at
http://tinyurl.com/cpd7sjv

COACHING & CONSULTING:
Go to http://www.EffectivenessPlus.com

www.ingramcontent.com/pod-product-compliance
Lightning Source LLC
Chambersburg PA
CBHW060507030426
42337CB00015B/1783